Dog Training 101

Dog Training 101

Step-by-Step Instructions for Raising a Happy, Well-Behaved Dog

Kyra Sundance

QUARRY

Brimming with creative inspiration, how-to projects, and useful information to enrich your everyday life, Quarto Knows is a favorite destination for those pursuing their interests and passions. Visit our site and dig deeper with our books into your area of interest: Quarto Creates, Quarto Cooks, Quarto Homes, Quarto Lives, Quarto Drives, Quarto Explores, Quarto Gifts, or Quarto Kids.

Inspiring | Educating | Creating | Entertaining

First Published in 2017 by Quarry Books, an imprint of The Quarto Group, 100 Cummings Center, Suite 265-D, Beverly, MA 01915, USA.
T (978) 282-9590 F (978) 283-2742 QuartoKnows.com

Quarry Books titles are also available at discount for retail, wholesale, promotional, and bulk purchase. For details, contact the Special Sales Manager by email at specialsales@quarto.com or by mail at The Quarto Group, Attn: Special Sales Manager, 100 Cummings Center, Suite 265-D, Beverly, MA 01915, USA.

10 9 8 7

ISBN: 978-1-63159-310-9

Digital edition published in 2017
eISBN: 978-1-63159-429-8

Library of Congress Cataloging-in-Publication Data available

Design: Sundance Media (sundancemedia.com)
Cover Image: Christian Arias, Slickforce Studios (slickforce.com)
Page Layout: Sundance Media
Photography: Christian Arias, Slickforce Studios
Illustration: Mattie Wells

Printed in Canada

DoMoreWithYourDog.com

CONTENTS

You have your friends, your work, your entertainment. Your dog has only you. You are his life, his love, his everything.
—Kyra Sundance

A dog family member can enrich our lives in so many ways: by giving us companionship and love, by engaging us in lighthearted play, and by generally spreading joy and enthusiasm.

But, in all honesty, they can also cause stress, frustration, and chaos in the household. We don't want that. The purpose of this book is to give you real-world tactics for correcting—or simply managing—these frustation-inducing behaviors. You will learn how to establish room boundaries that your dog is not allowed to cross (page 72), how to teach your dog to respect the children and other animals in the household (pages 30 to 33), and how to feed multiple dogs in a controlled way (page 68). You will learn how to correctly address your dog's fear or aggression issues by using methods of counterconditioning and positive redirection. And you will learn to teach your dog basic commands such as "come," "go to your spot," and "drop it."

In this book, you will use positive training methods to build a joyful relationship with your dog, where he is a willing partner in the training process. Training builds relationships by deepening communication pathways, trust, and mutual respect. It offers a way to bond with your dog as you strive toward common goals. The trust and cooperative spirit developed through this process will last a lifetime.

I hope this book helps to enhance your relationship with your dog and encourages you to "Do More With Your Dog!®"

Chapter 1

Before Your Dog Comes Home

Prepare

for success by using the tips in this chapter to arrange your home environment before your new family member arrives. The environment consists not only of the physical items in and around your home but also the rule structure and emotional vibe.

Prepare for your dog's arrival by addressing changes to your home's physical environment in order of priority. The first priority is to **secure** the perimeter, so your new dog cannot accidentally get out.

Next, review your property with an eye for **safety**. Look for things your dog may swallow, step on, knock over, get cut on, jump off of, etc.

Our next priority is to make your dog's environment **hygienic**. Clean, disinfect, and remove trash and waste.

And lastly, make your dog's new home **comfortable**. This includes temperature control, soft bedding, and enough space to exercise.

PREPARE YOUR DOG'S ENVIRONMENT

Congratulations on your new canine family member! Our primary responsibilty as pet parents is to ensure our dog's safety, security, and comfort. Take some time to address each of these responsibilities before your dog arrives.

Step 1: Secure the Perimeter

Your first priority in surveying your dog's new enviroment will be to secure the perimiter—both from your dog escaping and also from animal and people intruders.

Large dogs require a fence of 6 feet (2m) high, though some dogs may even be able to scale that height. Dogs are innovative and may find an object to act as a step to jumping over the fence.

Dogs frequently dig underneath fences.

A double fence is helpful in your entrance, so that your dog cannot sneak by you when the first fence is accidentally opened.

Step 2: Safety

Check the environment for anything that may injure your dog. This includes poisonous substances and foods (see page 170), loose nails, electrical cables, sharp sticks or bones that your dog may swallow (see page 168), other animals such as raptors (which will attack small dogs), coyotes, or raccoons. Check for drowning hazards such as a pool that has vertical sides that your dog may not be able to climb out of. A dog may go into a crawl space under the house and become trapped or encounter a snake.

Temperature hazards are a threat to all dogs. Your dog needs shade and fresh water in the summer and a warm, heated dog house in the cold. For the safety and comfort of your dog, he should sleep indoors at night.

Step 3: Hygiene

Once your dog's environment is secure and safe, we address cleanliness. Dogs can transmit diseases to each other via common water bowls and via feces in common potty areas. In a multi-dog environment, the kennel floors should be cleaned and disinfected daily.

Water bowls must be cleaned daily to kill bacteria and algae. Dog food should be stored in an air-tight container to keep it fresh and free from ants and bugs.

Your dog's bedding and toys must be washed regularly (in the washing machine or dishwasher).

Clean up trash and pet waste daily.

Step 4: Comfort

Now that our dog is safe and healthy, we turn our attention to his comfort. A dog should have soft bedding, shade, and enough space to exercise. A dedicated potty area with grass or dirt would be ideal for your dog.

Your dog may appreciate a coat in the winter and booties if there is ice on the ground.

TO PREPARE FOR YOUR DOG'S ARRIVAL

PREPARE YOUR MINDSET

Dogs can be frustrating. Dogs can be manipulative, and can take advantage of a situation. Instead of flying by the seat of your pants, be prepared with your calm, self-assured attitude by reviewing the following rules:

Rule 1: Be Fair

Treat your dog fairly by having rules that are specific, clear, and achievable—and consequences that are fair and predictable.

Rule 2: Be Consistent

Be clear about what you want; ask for it in a consistent way; and don't go back on your decisions.

Rule 3: Motivate with Positive Reinforcement

Build a dog's motivation to please by rewarding his good behavior. Focus on solutions rather than problems. Help the dog develop a pattern of success and good behavior.

Rule 4: Attention Is a Reward

Recognize your attention toward your dog as the powerful reward that it is. Use it as a payoff for your dog's good behavior and withdraw it as a consequence for his inappropriate behavior.

Rule 5: Discipline

Discipline is not punishment and is not hurtful; it is the compassionate enforcement of fair rules. Discipline is a clear and consistent structure for you and your dog to understand expectations and consequences.

Rule 6: Forgive

Don't hold a grudge—deal with misbehavior and let it go. Always give your dog another chance to be a "good dog."

PREPARE EVERYONE IN THE HOUSE FOR THEIR NEW RESPONSIBILITIES

Within your family, discuss who is responsible for the new dog or puppy before he arrives. The dog will not only need someone to take him outside on walks, feed him, and play with him, but he will also need love and acceptance from all members of the household.

ASSEMBLE YOUR SUPPORT TEAM

Although it doesn't need to be right away, you'll eventually want to enlist some people to support your dog's needs. Here are a few roles that you may need to fill:

☐ **Veterinarian**
Your dog will need routine vaccinations throughout his life.

☐ **Emergency Animal Hospital**
Know the closest emergency facilities that have a vet after hours.

☐ **Pet Insurance**
Research medical insurance for your dog.

☐ **Groomer**
Stay on site while your dog is being groomed so you are aware of what is going on.

☐ **Pet Sitter**
Professional pet sitters will come to your home or even live at your home while you are on vacation.

☐ **Boarding Kennel**
Ask quesions about how the dogs interact with each other and how often dog fights occur.

☐ **Dog Training Lessons**
Even brand new puppies should be enrolled in training classes.

☐ **Trusted Friend**
Designate a contact in case of emergency.

GATHER YOUR DOG'S GEAR

Provide a stable environment for your dog by having all of his gear in place before he arrives. Here are some items to consider:

Food

- [ ] **Dog Food**
  Start with food he is used to. Preferably switch to a food with no corn or grains.

- [ ] **Dog Treats / Biscuits**
  With no sugar or corn syrup or cane syrup

- [ ] **Edible Bones**
  Do not give your dog real bones, as it is common for the sharp pieces to get caught in a dog's mouth or throat. Edible dog bones are long-lasting chews.

- [ ] **Rawhides**
  Having rawhide chews available will usually keep a dog from chewing your shoes and furniture. Be aware, some dogs will swallow big chunks of rawhide which can lodge in their intestines.

- [ ] **Fresh Water**
  If your dog is outside, there are guzzler attachments for your water spigot that your dog can push to release fresh water.

- [ ] **Bowls for Food and Water**
  Stainless steel bowls resist bacteria.

Collars & Leashes

- [ ] **Collar**
  A flat, buckle collar is the safest. Breakaway collars reduce the risk of accidental strangulation. Never leave a dog unattended in a slip collar or chain collar. Be aware that dogs sometimes catch their collar when they jump up on chain-link fences.

- [ ] **Leash**
  A braided leather leash or a leash with some girth will be much easier to hold when your dog pulls than a flat nylon leash.

- [ ] **Harness or Head Halter**
  For dogs that pull or dogs that have sensitive necks, you may wish to use a harness or head halter instead of a collar.

- [ ] **Car Seatbelt or Confinement**
  For safety, dogs should be restrained in the car by a seatbelt, a gate, or inside a dog crate. It is illegal for a dog to ride unconfined in the back of a pickup truck.

- [ ] **ID Tags**
  Ideally tags should be permanently rivited to every one of your dog's collars.

- [ ] **Microchip**
  Your vet can implant an identifying microchip the size of a grain of rice between your dog's shoulders. All vets and animal shelters scan unknown animals for these chips.

- [ ] **Dog License**
  All dogs are required to have a county-issued dog license. The dog is required to have a rabies vaccination in order to be licensed.

- [ ] **Muzzle**
  A basket muzzle can be used to safeguard an aggressive dog and is also useful in emergency situations; if a dog is in pain, he may bite someone who tries to touch him.

- [ ] **Cone / Elizabethan Collar**
  A cone on your dog's neck is used to prevent him from licking a wound.

Grooming Tools

☐ **Dog Shampoo**
Human shampoo is too harsh for dogs.

☐ **Nail Trimmers**
Either dog trimmers or a Dremmel

☐ **Ear Cleaning Solutions**
Ear infections are common. Routine flushing will reduce ear wax.

☐ **Brush**
A soft rubber brush for short hair; a bristle brush for long hair

☐ **Dog Toothbrush and Toothpaste**
Small breed dogs may lose their teeth if not brushed. Rubber finger-glove toothbrushes work well. Dog toothpaste is often flavored with liver or peanut butter.

☐ **Chemical Deodorizer for Potty Accidents**
Dogs are more likely to urinate in an area which has urine odor.

☐ **First-Aid Supplies**
Antiseptic, Neosporin, anti-diarrhea medicine, Benedryl

☐ **Pickup Bags**
Biodegradable options available

☐ **Waste Can**
A shovel and can for dog waste

Beds & Crates

☐ **Dog Crate**
Large enough for your dog to stand up and fully turn around in

☐ **Beds in Several Rooms**
Soft, clean dog beds give your dog an appropriate place to be.

☐ **Playpen / Ex-Pen**
These portable pens can temporarily contain your dog while allowing him more room than a crate.

Training Tools

☐ **Bitter Apple Spray**
Spray on objects to prevent your dog from chewing them.

☐ **Pedestal**
A small, raised platform which becomes your dog's home base

☐ **Toys**
A chew toy, food dispensing toy, rip-apart toys, tug toy

Chapter 2

Steps for a Smooth Transition

Welcome to the family! Bringing a new dog into the household is a big transition; for both the dog and for your current family. Set your dog up for success by easing him into his new life in a way that reduces anxiety yet also establishes rules and boundaries.

Your primary job when bringing home your new dog is to ensure his security, safety, and mental well-being.

Remember, being too lenient with your dog is not going to damage your dog permanently; you can always rein him in later. However, being too harsh with your dog—dominating him or causing him fear—can injure your dog for a lifetime. Be kind and gentle and set the tone for a loving relationship.

In this chapter, we gently and confidently establish boundaries for your dog with a collar, leash, crate, and potty spot.

Introducing the Collar or Harness

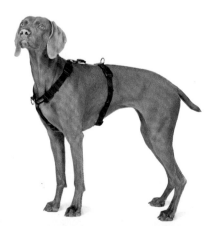

BEFORE YOU START

Use a flat-buckle collar to first introduce your dog to wearing a collar. Certain breeds with delicate necks (such as sighthounds) need a wider collar. Never leave a dog unattended in a slip collar (chain collar) due to the risk of strangulation. Be cautious of hanging identification tags that could get caught on something.

TROUBLESHOOTING

WHY SHOULD I CONSIDER A HARNESS INSTEAD OF A COLLAR?

Some small breed dogs with protruding eyeballs can strain so hard at a collar that their eyes can bleed or come out of their sockets. A harness (especially a front-clip harness) can give you more control over a dog pulling on his leash. A strong, intense dog can injure his neck or trachea by lunging on his leash while wearing a collar. Harnesses are useful in constraining your dog in a seat belt and in maneuvering him while swimming.

TIP! Buy multiple ID tags and attach them permanently to each of your dog's collars.

TEACH IT:

A dog's collar or harness is not only a useful tool, but also a symbol of his domestication. This is your first chance to make a positive and compassionate impression on your dog. Don't trick him, force him, or cause him to distrust you.

COLLAR

1. Fill your dog's rubber toy (like a Kong) with peanut butter to distract him.

2. Give him a pleasant neck scratching to get him used to you touching his neck.

3. While he's still licking peanut butter, buckle the collar around his neck.

4. Immediately take him on a walk or play ball or do something to get his mind onto something besides the collar.

HARNESS

1. Slip the harness first over your dog's head.

2. Line up the backpiece. Depending on the harness, you may have to lift one foot through the armhole. Buckle on the opposite side.

WHAT TO EXPECT: Most dogs accept a collar pretty easily, but some dogs will freeze in place. Distraction is usually your best strategy.

STEPS:

COLLAR

1 Give your dog a peanut-butter filled Kong toy.

2 Scratch his neck.

3 Buckle the collar.

4 Immediately distract him with an activity.

HARNESS

1 Slip the opening over your dog's head.

2 Pull one arm though the armhole and buckle the other side.

Introducing the Leash

TEACH IT:

A leash physically ties you and your dog together. It acts not merely as a restraint, but as a line of communication between the two of you. Treat it with respect and understand that a yank or a jerk on this line are the same as a smack: not so much a communication as a frustrated attempt at control.

1   Introduce the leash at chowtime, when your dog is intently focused on something else. Attach the leash and let it drop. By pairing the leash with food, the dog develops a positive association of the leash.

2   Some dogs react to a leash by freezing and refusing to move. In this instance, use treats and encourage your dog to walk just a few steps toward you. When he does, reward him with a walk.

3   When a leash is attached, some dogs act like a fish caught on a line and buck. You don't want the fear and frustration to escalate, but neither do you want the dog to be rewarded for bucking by having his leash removed (as that would essentially teach him to buck every time the leash is attached). Instead, try to distract your dog with food, play, or a walk.

WHAT TO EXPECT: Most dogs accept the leash fairly easily. If your dog is one of the exceptions that bucks or freezes, you can expect this to last for only a few minutes, and it should wear off in a few days.

BEFORE YOU START

Introduce the leash in a confined space, as you don't want your dog to freak out and run away with the leash still chasing him!

TROUBLESHOOTING

HOW SOON AFTER GETTING MY DOG SHOULD I INTRODUCE THE LEASH?

The first day is a little overwhelming, but by the second day your dog should be ready for the leash.

TIP! Never wrap the leash around your hand, as this is a frequent cause of injuries and broken bones.

STEPS:

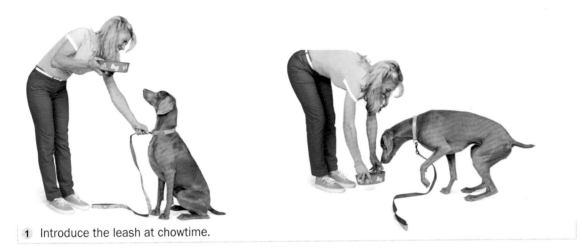

1. Introduce the leash at chowtime.

2. If your dog freezes, encourage him with treats. Reward with a walk.

3. If your dog bucks, try to distract him instead of removing the leash.

Crate Training / Bedtime

TEACH IT:

Crate training is the process of teaching a dog to accept a crate as a familiar and safe location. Dogs are den-dwelling animals and a crate can become a den substitute, helping the dog feel secure, safe, and comfortable. A crate is useful in travel, not only to keep your dog safe and confined but also to help him feel secure in an unfamiliar location. When bringing a dog into your home, a crate can give your dog time to adjust to new surroundings and can ease the transition from one family to another.

1   Make your dog's crate comfortable. You might include some bedding material from his previous home, water, toys, a peanut butter-filled Kong, a soothing ticking clock, and a hot water bottle. Place the crate next to your bed for the first few nights.

2   Before bedtime, try to have your dog tired and pottied. You may wish to withhold water for the last hour of the night.

3   Put some treats inside the crate and allow your dog to approach the crate on his own. (Never push a dog toward a feared object, as it will increase his fear.)

4   Close the crate door and settle quietly, while letting your dog know that you are still in the room with him.

5   Don't let your dog out of the crate while he is barking, as this would teach him to bark when he wants to come out.

6   Instead, wait until your dog gives a few moments of silence and reward that by opening the crate door.

WHAT TO EXPECT: The vast majority of dogs quickly grow to love their crate and seek it out when they wish some alone time (or a reprieve from household chaos or children). Allow your dog this space and do not bother him when he chooses to go in there.

BEFORE YOU START
Choose a cue for going into the crate, such as "kennel up!"

TROUBLESHOOTING
MY DOG IS WHINING. I THINK HE HAS TO GO POTTY.
If you've withheld water at the end of the night and pottied him right before bed, your dog or puppy should be able to spend all night in his crate. But be careful ... he'll want to potty the second he comes out!

TIP! For puppies, purchase a large crate, but section it off to a smaller area until they grow into it.

STEPS:

1 Make your dog's crate comfortable.

2 Have your dog tired out and pottied before bedtime.

3 Put some treats inside. Allow your dog to approach it on his own.

4 Close the door and settle quietly in the room.

5 Don't open the crate door while your dog is barking.

6 Reward his silence with freedom.

Potty Training

TEACH IT:

The key to potty training is to get as many successful episodes as possible. If your dog potties in the house, consider it a mistake on your part for not managing the routine well enough.

1. Take your dog on a leash to the designated potty spot. With too much freedom, your dog will be continually interested in sniffing and investigating and will not potty. Plant your feet so your dog cannot range far. Say, "Go potty" every once in a while; over time your dog will come to understand this instruction.

2. Praise your dog with "Good go potty" when he does.

3. If you're on a walk and your dog goes potty, do not immediately turn around to walk home as this would essentially teach your dog his pottying is causing the walk to end. Instead, after he potties, continue forward for a while before returning home.

4. There are predictable times when your dog will be likely to potty; be prepared at these times to take him outside to be successful. Those times include: immediately after coming out of his crate, first thing in the morning, after a meal, and when he wakes from a nap.

5. If your dog has an accident in the house, do not punish your dog. Clean the area and deodorize it to make it less likely that your dog will go in that same spot again. If you catch your dog in the act, take him out immediately to finish pottying outside.

WHAT TO EXPECT: Small breed dogs generally require more consistency in order to potty train. Puppies, although they may seem to be potty trained in a few weeks, will usually continue to have occasional accidents until the age of one or two.

BEFORE YOU START

Dogs are more likely to go in an area that is clean, grassy, and has few distractions.

TROUBLESHOOTING

MY DOG WON'T GO OUTSIDE IF IT'S RAINING / COLD.

Many small breed dogs are reluctant to go outside in bad weather. You can use a turf potty box near the door or even potty pads in a plastic kiddie pool.

TIP! Puppies need to go out every 90 minutes. They may potty a dozen times a day.

STEPS:

1 Plant your feet.

2 Praise your dog for pottying.

3 If you're on a walk, do not turn around immediately after your dog potties.

4 There are predictable times when your dog will be likely to want to go potty. Be ready.

5 Clean and deodorize accident spots.

Chapter 3

Introducing Your Family

Greeting

a family member for the first time can be a pleasant experience ... or a chaotic one. Follow the steps in this chapter to teach your dog his name and teach him how to politely interact with the human and animal members of your family.

Set the tone from the start—this is a harmonious household. Your dog must understand that he may not bully or overrun your child nor the cat.

Teach your dog how to interact calmly with other animal family members.

Teach the children in your household how to act respectfully toward the dog and how to de-escalate a potentially excitable situation.

Teach Your Dog His Name

BEFORE YOU START

Decide on ONE name for your dog, and say it in a consistent voice.

TROUBLESHOOTING

I JUST ADOPTED MY DOG. CAN I CHANGE HER NAME?

Yes. It takes about two months of consistent use for your dog to become very familiar with her name.

TIP! You want your dog to have a positive association with her name, so only use it in a happy voice in conjunction with good things. If you have to reprimand your dog, simply say "no!" or "cut it out!" without using her name.

TEACH IT:

Many dog owners take it for granted that their dog knows her own name, but that is not always the case. Make an effort to ensure your dog knows her name.

1. When your dog is walking around, say her name in a happy voice.

2. When she gives you her attention, give her a treat. Increase the distance so she has to come to you to get the treat.

3. Pair her name with other positive experiences: "Kimba, chowtime," "Kimba, fetch," "Kimba, go for a walk."

WHAT TO EXPECT: The more rewarding of an experience to attach to your dog's name, the faster she will learn to respond to it. Every time you have something good to give her, insert her name into the event.

STEPS:

1 Say your dog's name in a happy voice.

2 When she looks at you, give her a treat.

3 Pair her name with other positive experiences.

Teach Respect for Other Pets

BEFORE YOU START

Your dog will want to sniff the cat. Instead, give him the cat blanket to investigate. This will reduce the excitement of meeting the live cat.

TROUBLESHOOTING

MY CAT IS MEAN TO MY DOG!

It is not uncommon for a dog to wind up at the vet's office due to a cat scratch on his eye. If your pets aren't going to be friends, then they need to keep their distance from each other. Call your dog away from the cat whenever she approaches. The serious tone of your voice will let your dog know this is a household rule.

TIP! Give your cat some places where only he can access, such as a small cat door into the laundry room.

TEACH IT:

Your dog must respect the other pets in your household and not cause them fear.

1. Let your cat feel more in control by being higher up. When she is in a calm mood, allow your leashed dog to investigate the cat.

2. If your dog is too interested, redirect her attention back to you by offering a treat or gentle (not excited) cooing.

3. Be in control of the situation. If the cat is hissing or showing signs of stress, remove your dog and try again later.

4. Use a soft but firm voice to tell her to "be gentle."

WHAT TO EXPECT: Some dog breeds were bred as hunters and will have the instinct to chase or shake the cat. Even these natural instincts can be kept in check, however, with firm and consistent enforcement of house rules. It will be far easier for the animals to control their excitement indoors, rather than outdoors.

STEPS:

1 Allow your cat to have the height advantage.

2 If your dog is too interested, redirect her attention toward you.

3 Be in control. Remove your dog if things escalate.

4 Tell your dog to "be gentle."

Teach Respect for Children

BEFORE YOU START

Have a talk with the child about respectful, kind behavior toward your dog and safety measures.

TROUBLESHOOTING

MY DOG IS NOT OBEYING THE CHILD.

Try having the child stand on a box. Height implies authority.

TIP! Respect is a two way street. In order for your dog to respect the child, the child must be kind and respectful to the dog as well.

TEACH IT:

Your dog should respect every member of your family, including the children. Help your dog understand this by backing up your child's commands.

1. Stand behind the child as she gives the dog a command that the dog knows well, such as "sit." Have the child use strong, straight body posture and a clear, commanding voice.

2. If your dog does not obey the child, immediately back the child up by giving the same command to your dog.

3. When your dog obeys, let the child give her the treat. Food is power, and by letting the child control the food, you are increasing her power.

4. Walking a dog is another way of demonstrating leadership. Have the child walk the dog, as you follow behind, ready to help out if needed.

WHAT TO EXPECT: Look for opportunities every day where the child can give a command and a reward to your dog. In just a few weeks you'll see a big difference in how your dog responds.

STEPS:

1 Stand behind your child as she gives the command.

2 Back the child up by giving the command yourself.

3 Let the child give the treat.

4 Walk behind the child as she walks your dog.

Safety Around Children

TEACH IT:

What can a child do when a dog starts jumping on her? Or nipping at her or scratching her? How should a child act when approached by an unfamiliar or scary dog? Prepare your child with the "be a tree" technique of disengaging the dog.

1. Dogs respond to energy with energy. To de-escalate the situation, have the child plant her roots.
   [This will stop the child from running. Running engages the dog's chase drive.]

2. Fold in her branches.
   [This stops flailing arms, and also puts the child's hands where the dog can sniff them. The child's hands should be open, so the dog knows she is not gripping a treat.]

3. And look down at her leaves.
   [Eye contact can be confrontational. When the child looks at her hands, she cannot make eye contact with the dog.]

4. If the dog knocks the child down, she should then "be a rock."

WHAT TO EXPECT: The "be a tree" technique is extremely effective. The more often the child uses it with your dog, the faster your dog will learn to disengage.

BEFORE YOU START

Have the child practice this technique without the dog. That way it will become second nature to perform when necessary.

TROUBLESHOOTING

HOW OLD DOES A CHILD HAVE TO BE TO USE THIS TECHNIQUE?

Very young children, even toddlers, can use this technique effectively.

TIP! Food can easily trigger a dog and lead to aggressive or pushy behavior. Be cautious of letting a child near a dog with food.

STEPS:

1. Plant your roots …

2. Fold in your branches …

3. Look at your leaves.

4. If you get knocked down, be a rock.

Chapter 4

Acclimating Your Dog

to His New World

Discovery of new people, animals, objects, and experiences can be exciting and elating for a dog but can sometimes also be scary. Introduce these new things to your dog in a way that feels safe and controlled and gives him confidence to handle the situation.

Whether it be her first visit to the vet, first nail trimming, or first car ride, your dog will be anxious with these new experiences. Follow the steps in this chapter to introduce each new experience in a slow, controlled manner, which is associated with a positive outcome. A little extra time in the beginning will pave the way for a lifetime of confidence and healthy curiosity.

Set the tone for each new experience by portraying a calm confidence in your surroundings. Remember, your dog will do what you expect her to do, so control your thoughts and visualize the experience you wish to happen.

Socializing

TEACH IT:

Socializing means exposing your dog to new people, animals, objects, and experiences. Approach each new experience slowly, and give treats or praise and petting to give it a positive association. There are hundreds of new things you can expose your dog to, but listed here are a few examples.

1. ELEVATORS. It will probably be a challenge to even get your dog to set foot inside an elevator, so practice just that first step with some treats.

2. CLOTHES. A veterinary cone is used to prevent the dog from fussing with a sore spot. Acclimate your dog to this tool by giving her treats when you put it briefly on her.

3. UNSTABLE SURFACES. Try something simple like laying a board on the ground on top of a tiny pebble. Can you tempt your dog to step on this unstable surface?

4. PEOPLE. This step is often underestimated, but a dog needs to be exposed to a wide variety of people.

5. LOUD SOUNDS. When you have a new puppy in the house, don't be reluctant to make loud sounds. So long as your puppy is not too spooked, go ahead and slam those cupboard doors, rattle pots and pans, and ring the doorbell. This will desensitize your puppy to loud sounds.

6. ANIMALS. Horses, cats, reptiles, birds, and livestock will each present a novel experience for your dog.

WHAT TO EXPECT: Dogs vary widely in their confidence with new experiences. A lot of this variance is due to genetics. Socialization will have the greatest benefit to a dog during puppyhood, especially in their first four months of life.

BEFORE YOU START

Know the signs of stress: trembling, cowering, tucked tail, lowered head, lip licking, panting, scratching, hiding.

TROUBLESHOOTING

WHAT DO I DO IF MY DOG IS AFRAID OF SOMETHING?

Never push a dog toward a feared object, as it will increase his fear. See the chapter "Getting Braver" (page 108).

TIP! The more new experiences that your dog gets used to, the faster he will adjust to each new experience thereafter.

STEPS:

1. Elevators: revolving doors, automatic doors

2. Clothes: cone, coat, booties

3. Unstable surfaces: wobble board

4. People: children, wheelchair, cane

5. Loud sounds: doorbell, doors slamming, siren

6. Animals: smell and movement

Car

BEFORE YOU START

Research the applicable laws in your county and state. It is commonly unlawful to have a dog leashed in the back of a pickup and unlawful to have a dog alone in a car for any duration of time, in any temperature.

TROUBLESHOOTING

HELP, MY DOG GETS CAR SICK!

Dogs may drool or vomit due to anxiety or to motion sickness. Limit your dog's food consumption before going on a car trip. Consider asking your veterinarian about an FDA-approved medication for canine motion sickness.

TIP! The first you time you introduce the car, just practice getting in, sitting there for a minute, and getting out (without ever moving the car).

TEACH IT:

Every dog should be accustomed to riding in a car. For the safety of your dog and of all the travelers on the road, restrain your dog inside a crate or with the use of a harness and seat belt.

1. Put a secure harness on your dog (page 18). Test that he cannot slip out of it by walking backward.

2. Buckle the harness loop through the seat belt.

3. Or, put a crate inside your car. A squeak toy, chew toy, or peanut butter-filled toy will occupy your dog.

4. Commercial car ramps can help your dog walk into the car. If you lift your dog, gather her by her shoulders and rump to avoid putting pressure on her chest or stomach.

WHAT TO EXPECT: Introducing this experience to a puppy will be much easier than introducing it to a mature dog.

STEPS:

1 Attach and test the harness.

2 Buckle it through the seat belt.

3 Use a crate inside the car.

4 Lift your dog by avoiding pressure.

First Vet's Office Visit

BEFORE YOU START

It can be helpful to start with a pleasant pet store visit before you attempt the scarier vet's office visit.

TROUBLESHOOTING

MY DOG REFUSES TO ENTER THE OFFICE.

Never force your dog toward a feared object, as it will only increase her fear. Use treats to coax your dog slowly (page 112).

MY DOG IS SHAKING AND PANTING EXCESSIVELY.

This is not uncommon. Don't overly coddle your dog; instead portray confidence and calmness in the situation.

TIP! The grass surrounding the vet's office has been pottied on by many sick animals. Avoid letting your dog step on those areas.

TEACH IT:

The vet's office can be a scary place for a dog; it has slippery floors (see page 124), other dogs who may be in pain, and "fear pheromone" odors. Acclimate your dog to the vet's office before he needs it, so he'll start off with a positive association.

1. Stop by the vet's office on a random day, when you don't have an appointment. Your dog will be anxious; take your time.

2. Give your dog treats to distract him from his anxiety.

3. There is often a biscuit jar on the reception desk. Let the staff person give your dog a treat.

4. Keep it short and upbeat. Leave the vet's office on a high note. What fun that was!

WHAT TO EXPECT: Stop by the vet's office a few times before the need arises. When it's time for your dog's first appointment, it will be "no big deal."

STEPS:

1 Stop by the vet's office when you don't have an appointment.

2 Distract your dog with treats.

3 Get a biscuit from the reception desk.

4 Keep your first visit short.

Permitting Petting and Affection

TEACH IT:

Part of socializing your dog is helping her become comfortable with your touch and physical manipulation. Touch and petting are a bonding activity and will improve your overall relationship.

1. Let your dog nibble a treat or lick some peanut butter from your hand as you gently stroke her. She will start to pair these two pleasant experiences together.

2. Rub her ears. This will be useful when you later clean her ears.

3. Pet her paws and gently rub your palm against her pads. This will also prepare her for nail trimming.

4. Briefly lift her lip to inspect her teeth. When she is more secure, we'll begin brushing her teeth.

5. Practice the "settle" technique; ease your dog onto your outstretched legs and gently say "Settle ... settle ..."

WHAT TO EXPECT: Some dogs enjoy affection and others have to learn to love it. Try not to be offended if your dog is not a natural cuddler.

BEFORE YOU START
Attempt affection at the end of the day, when your dog is tired and there is less "interesting stuff" going on.

TROUBLESHOOTING

MY DOG FLATTENS HER EARS OR GROWLS AT ME!
Do not make this a battle. Your dog is telling you that she does not want to be touched. Let her go and attempt it again another day. Perseverance is the way to win her over.

TIP! Attempt affection in very short spurts. If your dog struggles to get away, release her immediately.

STEPS:

1 Use peanut butter to introduce petting.

2 Rub your dog's ears.

3 Smooth her paws.

4 Lift her gums.

5 Practice the "settle" technique.

Nail Trimming

TEACH IT:

When a dog's nails are too long they prevent the dog from standing properly flat-footed, which can eventually lead to injury or arthritis. It is especially important to keep a puppy's nails trimmed. Trimming your dog's nails will be a lifelong task, so approach it slowly and correctly so your dog will not fear it. The following steps may take a week or more to work through.

1. Gently pick up and handle your dog's paw while giving her treats. If she struggles, release her paw (but she only gets treats while her paw is in your hand).

2. Touch each nail with the clippers.

3. While holding your dog's paw, clip a wooden matchstick. This will accustom your dog to the sound of the clip.

4. After every matchstick clip, give your dog a treat.

5. When your dog is ready, clip the tiniest bit off one nail, and immediately praise and treat.

WHAT TO EXPECT: This will be a long, frustrating process but worth the work. Make it your goal to simply TOUCH each nail with the clippers.

BEFORE YOU START

You'll need dog nail clippers, wooden matches, and small treats.

TROUBLESHOOTING

CAN I LEASH MY DOG? SHE IS TRYING TO RUN AWAY.

You can leash her on a long leash to prevent her from running off, but you must give her enough lead so she doesn't feel trapped and resort to panic-biting.

TIP! Is your puppy biting your hand? Wear gloves.

STEPS:

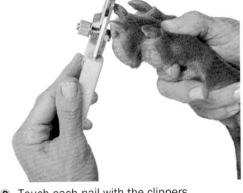

1 Give treats while holding her paw.

2 Touch each nail with the clippers.

3 Clip a matchstick to imitate the sound.

4 After every matchstick clip, give a treat.

5 Trim one nail and give a treat.

Chapter 5

Basic Commands

Training

Training your dog is part of loving your dog, as it gives her the tools and understanding to be a "good dog." Training gives your dog access to more freedoms, as she is no longer a prisoner of her own misbehavior and will be able to go more places with you.

The foundation behaviors contained in this chapter will come in useful for the rest of your dog's life in a variety of ways. They are the basis of many skills we will be learning in this book, such as boundary training to direct your dog to stay out of the kitchen or how to politely greet visitors without jumping on them.

Teach using positive reinforcement by rewarding your dog for correct behavior instead of punishing her for incorrect behavior. And, as always, patience is key.

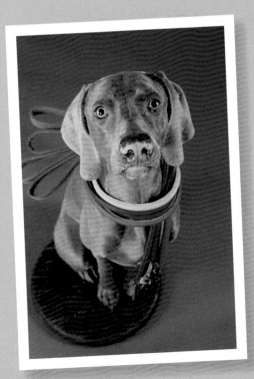

Focus / Eye Contact

BEFORE YOU START

First practice this skill when your dog is in a boring environment, without other dogs nearby.

TROUBLESHOOTING

MY DOG IS SMALL. SHOULD I SIT DOWN?

Eventually you shouldn't have to, but at the beginning it can be helpful to either sit or put your dog on a chair.

TIP! Before you throw your dog's ball or give him a treat, ask for a quick moment of eye contact.

TEACH IT:

All training begins with attention. And you don't have your dog's attention unless you have her eyes. Teach focus as the first step to all training.

1 Hold a treat to your dog's nose.

2 Say, "Focus ... focus ..." and draw the treat back to between your eyes. Keep eye contact with your dog the whole time. If she looks away, tell her to focus again.

3 After two seconds of eye contact, bring the treat straight back from your eyes to her mouth and let her have it. Over time, increase the duration of the eye contact.

4 Once your dog has the hang of this game, use just your pointed finger to draw her eye contact instead of the treat. Again, give a treat when she has held eye contact.

WHAT TO EXPECT: This is a pretty easy skill for a dog to learn and a useful one. With a week of practice, your dog will significantly improve her eye contact. Ask for no more than a few seconds of attention.

STEPS:

1 Hold a treat to your dog's nose.

2 Draw it back to your eyes.

3 Trace it forward to your dog's mouth.

4 Try it with a pointed finger.

Sit

BEFORE YOU START

Those treats will be extra appealing if you train BEFORE dinner time.

TROUBLESHOOTING

MY DOG NIPS AT MY HAND.
Hold your hand flat, with the treat wedged between two fingers. That way your dog won't be able to nip at anything.

TIP! Avoid pushing down on your dog's rump to get her to sit. Physically manipulating your dog into position teaches them to give up and be lead, rather than take an active role in problem solving.

TEACH IT:

A sit is often the first command a dog learns and is the start of a lifelong rapport with her owner. Have fun!

1. Hold a treat to your dog's nose to get her interest.

2. Say, "Sit" and move the treat slowly up and back. This will get her head pointed up, which should cause her rear to go down.

3. The instant her rear touches the floor, release the treat.

4. If your dog keeps backing up instead of sitting, try this same technique near a wall.

5. Finally, once your dog is getting good at this command, graduate to just using a raised palm as the hand signal for "sit." Continue to give a treat, as this will build a reward history with your dog.

WHAT TO EXPECT: Some dogs can be very squirmy at first, but once you get those first few sits things will rapidly progress. Be sure to give a treat for EVERY sit (as this will make learning go quicker).

STEPS:

1 Hold a treat to her nose.

2 Say, "Sit" and move the treat back to get her head up and rear down.

3 Release the treat.

4 Try this technique against a wall.

5 A raised palm becomes the hand signal for "sit."

Down

BEFORE YOU START

Dogs are more apt to lie down on a carpet or grass than on a hard floor.

TROUBLESHOOTING

MY DOG WILL NOT GO DOWN!

Try this: Sit on the floor with your feet flat and make a bridge with your knees. Use the treat to lure your dog under your knees. She will HAVE to go down to follow the treat!

TIP! It can help to kneel down on the floor with your dog. This will keep her eyes lower and not looking up at you.

TEACH IT:

Once your dog has learned to sit, teach her to lie down.

1. Start with your dog in a sit (page 52). Hold a treat to her nose.

2. Say "down" and move the treat to the floor. Experiment with sliding it either toward or away from your dog to get her to lie down.

3. If your dog stands up, try to slide the treat to a place that puts your dog in an uncomfortable position.

4. If your dog goes into a bow position, just hold the treat there until she gets tired and drops her rear. It can help to push the treat a tiny bit toward her nose.

5. As soon as she lies down, release the treat.

WHAT TO EXPECT: Depending on age, leg length, and other factors, your dog may be more or less likely to drop into a down. Most dogs will figure this skill out within two weeks.

STEPS:

1 In a sit, hold a treat to her nose.

2 Move it to the floor.

3 If your dog stands up, slide the treat to make her uncomfortable.

4 If she bows, hold the treat still or push it toward her until she drops.

5 When she drops, release the treat.

Stay

BEFORE YOU START
Teach your dog sit (page 52) and pedestal (page 110).

TROUBLESHOOTING

MY DOG KEEPS JUMPING OFF THE PEDESTAL.
You don't want your dog to have the experience of jumping off during a stay. Instead, lower your criteria for success by standing closer to your dog and having her stay for a shorter time. Only when she is repeatedly successful should you raise your criteria.

TIP! Keep your treat behind your back or in your pocket, so the sight of it doesn't tempt your dog off her pedestal.

TEACH IT:

A "stay" will be much easier to teach when you put your dog on a pedestal. This prop makes a natural barrier, which will help your dog be successful.

1. Put your dog on a pedestal such as a stool or an ottoman. Have her sit (page 52).

2. Present your palm in front of her face and say, "Stay."

3. Keeping your hand up the whole time, take one step back, then one step forward.

4. Walk ALL the way back to your dog before you present a treat. If you show her the treat too early, she will break her stay.

5. Once your dog is stable on the pedestal, try the stay on the floor. This will be harder for your dog, so ask her to stay for only a short time at a short distance.

WHAT TO EXPECT: Much of the success in this exercise comes from your strong body posture, eye contact, and hand signal. Stand up straight and solid, and your dog should respond accordingly.

STEPS:

1 Have her sit on a pedestal.

2 Present your palm and say, "Stay."

3 Keep your hand up. Take a step backward, then forward.

4 Walk all the way back before you give the treat.

5 Try it on the floor, going back to a shorter distance.

Come

TEACH IT:

A recall is the most useful command to teach to your dog. Reward your dog every single time she comes, whether it be with a treat or play or happy praise.

1. Get down on your knee and call your dog happily to "come!"

2. Don't show her the treat until she comes. Then break it out and surprise her with it. That way, she'll never know if you have a treat on you or not.

3. Crouch down and say, "Ready ... set ... come! Come! Come!" and run away from her, engaging her chase drive.

4. Help your dog learn this new word by saying "come" and using a leash to draw her in and help her be successful. Give her a treat when she gets to you, even if you guided her with the leash.

WHAT TO EXPECT: "Come" is a lifelong work in progress. By continuing to use treats and rewards, even sporadically, you will maintain your dog's motivation for coming to you.

STEPS:

1 Get down on your knee and call "come."

2 Pull out a surprise treat.

3 Engage your dog's chase drive.

4 Use a leash to guide your dog to success.

Drop It

BEFORE YOU START
Teach your dog the pedestal (page 110).

TROUBLESHOOTING

WON'T THIS ENCOURAGE MY DOG TO TAKE MORE SHOES, SO THAT SHE GETS MORE TREATS?

In fact, no. The dog will associate the treat with the pedestal and not with the shoe. What is more likely to happen is that when your dog wants a treat, you'll find her spontaneously jumping on her pedestal!

TIP! By using positive redirection we focus on ways we can reward good behavior instead of punish bad behavior. We help our dog be a "good dog."

TEACH IT:

Whether it be your shoe or your lunch bag or a dead rat, there are times when you're really going to want your dog to "drop it." We will combat this unwanted behavior by using positive redirection.

1. If you just yell "No!" your dog may run off. Instead, tell her what to do. Show her a treat and say, "Drop it."

2. Keep insisting that she drop it.

3. As soon as she does, send her enthusiastically to her pedestal. You can even run with her.

4. Reward her on the pedestal with a treat and praise.

WHAT TO EXPECT: By using positive redirection, we are redirecting the dog's attention from a bad behavior to a good behavior and then rewarding that good behavior. The dog does not get a treat for taking and then dropping the shoe; she gets a treat for going to the pedestal.

STEPS:

1 Show her a treat and say, "Drop it."

2 Keep insisting that she drop it.

3 Send her enthusiastically to her pedestal.

4 Reward her on the pedestal.

Leave It

BEFORE YOU START
Have a treat to put on the floor and an even better treat stashed in your pocket.

TROUBLESHOOTING

MY DOG NEVER STOPS GOING FOR THE TREAT!
Patience is key. If you block her enough times from getting the treat, she will eventually pause. Reward that slight pause.

TIP! You can also use "leave it" to keep your dog from approaching your sandwich, your cat, or anything else she is supposed to stay away from.

TEACH IT:
When you don't want your dog to eat something—or to even approach it—tell her to "leave it."

1   Put a treat on the ground. In an authoritative (but not loud) voice, tell her to "leave it." Keep your hand ready to cover the treat if she goes for it.

2   When she moves in on the treat, tell her "no" and cover the treat with your hand.

3   Repeat this process until your dog refrains from moving toward the treat for a second or two. Say, "Good" and hand her a different treat from your pocket.

WHAT TO EXPECT: Always reward your dog with a treat from your hand, rather than allowing her to take the treat from the floor, as allowing her to take the treat from the floor would teach her to fixate on that item. You instead want her to ignore that item.

STEPS:

1 Tell your dog to "leave it." Keep your hand ready.

2 When she moves, tell her "no" and cover the treat.

3 When she refrains, say, "Good" and hand her a treat from your pocket.

Chapter 6

Household Routines

KYRA SUNDANCE 2014

Home

life revolves around daily routines: cooking, eating, cleaning, and getting everyone out the door on time. The skills in this chapter will show you how to establish routines that foster a harmonious household.

The skills presented here are not behaviors that you train once, but rather manners that you practice every single day. In time, they become a pleasant dance for both you and your dog, as you progress through the steps of sitting before chowtime and having multiple dogs show restraint while their food bowls are being distributed. They are pleasant because they become anticipatory steps toward the known pleasant result.

Reduce the chaos in your household by teaching your dog to respect boundaries, both with spot training and with boundary training.

Sit Before Chowtime

BEFORE YOU START
Teach your dog to sit (page 52).

TROUBLESHOOTING

MY DOG JUST WON'T SIT.
Are you sure your dog knows the word "sit"? If you are sure she does, then try holding the food bowl above her head and moving toward her. This should cause her rear to drop, especially if her back is against a wall.

TIP! Don't "free feed" your dog. Instead, offer her a meal, and if she hasn't finished it in fifteen minutes, pick up the bowl.

TEACH IT:

It's never too early to start learning manners. Teach your polite pooch to sit before receiving her dinner.

1. Prepare your dog's meal and hold it out of her reach. Tell her to "sit." She may be so excited that she can't contain herself. Give her several chances to sit and help her by using the food bowl to lure her head up and back, causing her rear to drop.

2. If she does not sit, turn away and put the bowl out of her reach for a minute.

3. Try again a minute later. When your dog does finally sit, even for a second, mark that instant by saying, "Good."

4. Immediately put her bowl down as a reward for her politeness.

WHAT TO EXPECT: This exercise helps build good manners in your dog. It builds a habit of asking politely for her dinner rather than demanding it.

STEPS:

1 Use the food bowl to lure her head up.

2 If she doesn't sit, turn away.

3 When she does finally sit, say, "Good."

4 Immediately reward her for her politeness.

How to Feed Multiple Dogs

BEFORE YOU START
Teach your dogs to sit (page 52).

TROUBLESHOOTING

IT SEEMS UNFAIR THAT MY GOOD DOG HAS TO WAIT WHILE MY OTHER DOG TAKES FOREVER TO SIT!

Peer pressure is a powerful motivator. Observe carefully and you'll see hints that your good dog is giving signals to your other dog.

TIP! Have three or more dogs? Put the bowls five feet apart where you can stand in the middle in order to block a dog from going into another dog's food bowl.

TEACH IT:

Chowtime can be chaos in a multi-dog household. Have a plan for keeping control.

1. Hold both bowls and ask your dogs to "sit."

2. Keep at it until both (or all) of your dogs are sitting.

3. Put the bowls down and let them eat.

4. Sometimes dogs will try to invade each other's bowls. Stand between the bowls to act as a barrier.

WHAT TO EXPECT: Do this consistently, at every meal, and within a few weeks your dogs will be sitting even before you ask.

STEPS:

1 Ask your dogs to "sit."

2 Keep at it until both are sitting.

3 They are allowed to eat the second the bowls hit the ground.

4 Use your body as a barrier.

Ring the Bell to Go Out

TROUBLESHOOTING

**MY DOG RINGS THE BELL A
DOZEN TIMES A DAY!**

You are teaching your dog
that she has the ability to
communicate with you and that
you will respond to her polite
requests. It is important in the
beginning to respond every
time she rings the bell, because
if you don't, she'll learn that
you are non-responsive, and
she will no longer attempt
communication.

TIP! This skill works very well in
housetraining young puppies!

TEACH IT:

Teach your dog to ring a bell on the door to let you know
that she needs to go outside.

1   Hang a bell from a doorknob. Dab some peanut
    butter on the bell and encourage your dog to lick it by
    wiggling it and saying ,"Bell, get it!"

2   The instant your dog causes the bell to ring, say,
    "Good" and give her a treat from your hand. Repeat
    this several times in a row every day.

3   Get your dog's leash and get her excited to go for a
    walk. Stop at the door with the bell, encouraging her
    to ring it.

4   It may take a while, but as soon as she touches the
    bell, immediately open the door and take her outside.
    This time, the reward is access to the outdoors
    instead of a treat.

WHAT TO EXPECT: The more responsive you are to the
bells in the beginning, the quicker your dog will learn this
skill. Most dogs will start ringing the bell on their own
within a week.

STEPS:

1. Put some peanut butter on the bell. Say, "Bell, get it!"

2. When she rings it, say, "Good" and give her a treat.

3. Get your dog excited for a walk. Ask her to ring the bell.

4. Reward the bell ring by opening the door.

Boundary Training (Stay Out of Kitchen)

TEACH IT:

Teach your dog to respect a boundary, such as a doorway, the line between the tile and the carpet, or the edge of your lawn. In this example, we'll use the kitchen room boundary.

1. Set up a baby gate barrier at the kitchen doorway. Tell your dog to "stay." Walk away, but return immediately and give your dog a treat.

2. Replace the baby gate with a shorter barrier, such as a board and repeat the stay / treat exercise. Build up a longer "stay" duration.

3. Progress to using shorter and shorter barriers. If your dog hops the barrier, say "Out" and send her back (even if you have to walk her back) and try again. She only gets a treat when she does the exercise correctly.

4. Although theoretically a dog can be taught to respect a boundary that is just the edge of a carpet, it will be MUCH easier if you use a small barrier such as a 2" x 2" (5 cm x 5 cm) board.

5. Alternately, you can put a pedestal at the edge of the boundary. Dogs tend to be very successful at staying on a pedestal.

WHAT TO EXPECT: Depending on a dog's personality, results will vary. Some dogs are naturally obedient. Other dogs will push that limit and continually test you by stepping one inch over the boundary. Your power comes from your consistency.

BEFORE YOU START

Teach your dog to stay (page 56).

TROUBLESHOOTING

HOW LONG DO I HAVE TO KEEP GIVING TREATS?

In the learning stage, we use treats to motivate your dog to play along. After a few months you can wean off the treats and simply enforce the rule.

TIP! Reinforce the barrier with strong body language.

STEPS:

1 Set up a baby gate in the doorway and tell your dog to "stay." Give her a treat.

2 Progress to shorter barriers.

3 If she hops the barrier, say "Out" and send her back.

4 Always use a physical barrier of some sort.

5 Or use a pedestal at the edge of the room.

Spot Training

BEFORE YOU START
Teach your dog to lie down (page 54) and stay (page 56).

TROUBLESHOOTING

IS THERE JUST ONE "SPOT" OR MULTIPLE?
You can have a "spot" bed in each room. You can even take your spot with you on the road to give your dog security in an unfamiliar place.

TIP! You will have more success if you use a comfy dog bed, preferably one that is raised off the floor.

TEACH IT:
Teach your dog to go to her "spot" (her dog bed) and stay there.

1. Say, "Go to your spot!" and toss a treat onto your dog's bed.

2. Praise her while she is on the spot.

3. Have her lie down in her bed (as she is more likely to stay there in a down position).

4. Tell her "stay," back up a few steps, go forward, and reward her with a treat. Build up farther distance and longer stays.

5. If your dog breaks her stay and leaves her spot, immediately send her back. Ideally you can direct her back without a treat, but if there is no other way, you can use a treat to lure her onto the bed.

WHAT TO EXPECT: Dogs get the hang of spot training pretty easily.

STEPS:

1. Say, "Go to your spot!" and toss a treat on the bed.

2. Praise her on the bed.

3. Have her lie down.

4. "Stay," back up, step forward, and give a treat.

5. If your dog leaves her spot, send her back without using a treat.

Security Search of the House

BEFORE YOU START
Your dog will be more timid to enter a dark room. Use a remote switch to pre-light the house.

TROUBLESHOOTING

MY DOG ACTS LIKE SHE DOESN'T KNOW WHAT SHE'S LOOKING FOR.
She may not. But trust that while she is poking around, if she smells a person, she'll alert you!

TIP! Your dog can even "go search" your hotel room or any other new location.

TEACH IT:

Entering an empty house late at night? Train your dog to do a security sweep of the house to look for intruders.

1. Enter your house, point toward the first room and say, "Go search!"

2. When your dog returns to you, walk with her to the next room and direct her to "go search" that one. Repeat for every room.

3. After the entire house has been searched, praise your dog heartily (but don't give treats).

4. After about 20 days of guiding your dog to every room, she should start searching room by room by herself. Stand at the front door and keep coaching her from there to "go search."

WHAT TO EXPECT: Most dogs grow to enjoy this important job and do so readily even without treats.

STEPS:

1 Enter your house and say, "Go search!"

2 Walk her to the next room and direct her to "go search!"

3 After the last room, give enthusiastic praise.

4 Eventually you will be able to stand at the front door and send your dog to search the entire house.

Chapter 7

Take It Outside

Adventure

Adventure awaits, as you and your dog explore the town as well as nature hiking trails. Use the skills in this chapter to teach your dog to walk politely on-leash, to stay within range off-leash, and to come to you at the sound of a whistle.

It is sometimes taken for granted that a dog will obediently walk next to you, stay on the sidewalk and not in the street, and return to you when called. But in reality, these are all specific skills that need to be taught and rehearsed.

Rather than endure a lifetime of frustration and combat, make the commitment to teach your dog these outdoor skills. The rewards of smiles, tail wags, and enthusiastic play will be well worth the effort!

Leash Training (No Pulling)

BEFORE YOU START

Teach your dog to accept a collar (page 18) and leash (page 20).

TROUBLESHOOTING

SHOULD I USE TREATS?

There are no treats in this skill. The walk is the reward.

TIP! Never wind the leash around your wrist or hand. It is not uncommon to break bones this way.

TEACH IT:

Yes, you can actually teach your dog to walk without pulling! Your dog wants to move forward. We will only allow her to move forward when she has a slack leash. When the leash is taught ... we stop.

1 Start your walk with a slack leash.

2 As soon as your dog pulls ...

3 Stop in your tracks. Wait for as long as it takes until your dog makes the decision to slacken the leash.

4 As soon as the leash goes slack for one second, say, "Good."

5 Continue your walk.

WHAT TO EXPECT: The first day you attempt this method, you may not even make it to the end of your driveway. You can expect to be stopped every few seconds. This is normal. It WILL get better. Few people have the patience to stick with this plan, but it is an extremely effective method once taught.

STEPS:

1 Start your walk with a slack leash.

2 As soon as your dog pulls ...

3 Stop in your tracks.

4 As soon as the leash goes slack for one second, say, "Good"...

5 And continue your walk.

Curb Training (Sidewalk)

BEFORE YOU START
Teach your dog to walk on a loose leash (page 80).

TROUBLESHOOTING

MY DOG IS NOW SCARED OF MY FOOT.

Be delicate. You want to merely sweep that paw back where it belongs. This is not meant to be a punishment, but rather an instruction.

TIP! Keep a short leash so your dog stays easily within your reach if you need to do a foot sweep.

TEACH IT:

Train your dog to stay on the sidewalk and not step off the curb into the street.

1. Walk along the sidewalk with your body closer to the street than your dog's.

2. Veer out into the street. This will probably cause your dog to step into the street.

3. Try and catch the first foot that comes off the curb, and use your foot to sweep it back onto the sidewalk.

WHAT TO EXPECT: Dogs will usually learn to stay on a raised sidewalk after about a dozen walks.

STEPS:

1 Walk on the sidewalk, with your body nearer to the street.

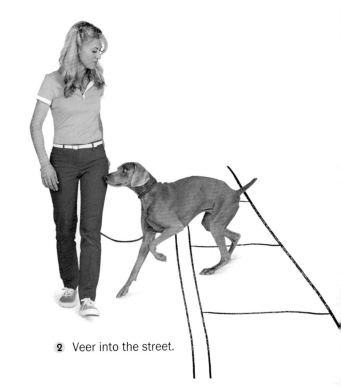

2 Veer into the street.

3 Sweep her paw back onto the sidewalk.

Running with Your Dog

TEACH IT:

Experience the adventure of running with your dog!

1. A harness keeps pressure off your dog's neck. A bungee or coil leash stays out from underfoot and lessens the jerkiness, making a smoother run for the both of you.

2. Never wind a leash around your wrist or hand, as this could result in a broken hand.

3. A beacon light keeps your dog visible at night.

4. A pop-up silicone, collapsible water bowl packs easily.

5. A short traffic lead keeps your dog close in crowded places or near a street. Position yourself on the side nearer to the street to protect your dog from cars.

6. If your dog is a puller, try attaching your leash to the front chest clip on her harness. When your dog tries to pull, she will be automatically redirected in an arc back toward you. This successfully and easily prevents her from pulling, with no effort on your part.

WHAT TO EXPECT: For even experienced runners, coordinating the leash and pace and direction can be a challenge and requires constant attention. The rewards of including your dog in healthy exercise are worth the trouble!

BEFORE YOU START

Heat is the biggest danger in running with your dog, and it will affect them before it affects you. Be observant; be smart.

TROUBLESHOOTING

HOW FAR CAN MY DOG RUN?

Look for warning signs: lagging on the leash, panting with tongue hanging out, laying down in the shade. Typically 6 miles (9.5 km) would be the max you'd take any dog.

TIP! Check your dog's pads after running. Avoid running on asphalt or abrasive surfaces.

STEPS:

1 Use a harness and bungee or coil leash.

2 Never wind a leash around your wrist.

3 A beacon light keeps your dog visible at night.

4 A pop-up silicone, collapsible water bowl packs easily.

5 A short traffic lead keeps your dog close near a street.

6 To easily prevent pulling, use a front-clip harness.

Off-Leash Hiking

TEACH IT:

Dogs love to run in forests and hiking trails, and most can be easily taught to stay close to you and to return to you when called. With training, your dog earns his independence.

1. Assemble your gear. A dog backpack is useful for carrying supplies and also makes your dog more visible. A collar bell will help you hear where your dog is. A dog bowl is easier for your dog to drink from than a sports bottle. A whistle can be heard by your dog from far away (see whistle training, page 88). Some dog treats in your pocket will help incentivize your dog to return to you when called.

2. Dogs pack together. Bringing a second dog will make it less likely for your dog to run off.

3. Keep your dog on leash for the first quarter of a mile (400 meters), until the initial excitement has tempered and you are away from the street. Make a habit of only releasing the leash when your dog has given you a slack line, so as not to reward him for pulling.

4. When your dog returns to you periodically to check in, give him a treat. This will prompt him to check in more often.

5. At the end of your hike, give your dog a "car cookie" treat. By doing so, in the future if your dog ever gets lost from you, chances are good that he will look for the car to get his treat!

WHAT TO EXPECT: Depending on the dog and the breed, some will range far and some will keep close to heel. Dogs learn very readily from other dogs, so hiking the first few times with an experienced companion will teach your dog the rules of this sport.

BEFORE YOU START
Consider the dangers in your specific area, such as coyotes, rattlesnakes, and cacti.

TROUBLESHOOTING

I'M AFRAID MY DOG WILL RUN OFF AND NOT COME BACK.
Having a stash of really good treats, and doling them out every few minutes, will almost assuredly keep your dog in close range.

TIP! GPS collars let you track your dog's location on your phone.

STEPS:

1. Backpack, collar bell,   water,   whistle,   treats.

2. Dogs pack together.

3. Release the leash only when your dog has given you slack.

4. When your dog checks in with you, give him a treat.

5. Reward the end of the hike with a "car cookie."

Whistle Training

BEFORE YOU START
Teach your dog to come
(page 58).

TROUBLESHOOTING

WHAT IF MY DOG IGNORES THE WHISTLE?

Just like with the "come" command, you don't want to let your dog get away with ignoring this cue. In general, stay in one place and keep whistling and calling to your dog. Persistence is a powerful thing. Let your dog know that however long it takes, you will not let this drop.

TIP! Do you have multiple dogs? Create a unique whistle pattern for each dog.

TEACH IT:

Whistle train your dog to come to the sound. This will come in handy on windy days or when your dog ranges far from you. A whistle allows any family member to be able to call your dog, as their "voices" will all sound the same.

1. Gently accustom your dog to the sound of the whistle. If she is fearful of it, pair the sound with treats.

2. When your dog is about 40 to 80 feet (12 to 24 meters) away from you, blow the whistle. Give a little variance to the whistle, as it will be easier for your dog to locate than a single, steady tone.

3. Immediately hold up a treat and excitedly call your dog. It's important to FIRST blow the whistle, AND THEN call your dog, as we always introduce the new cue before the known cue.

4. When your dog gets to you, give her the treat.

WHAT TO EXPECT: Dogs whistle train extremely easily and react to the whistle almost on the first try. For the most enthusiastic and consistent results, give a treat EVERY time your dog comes to your whistle sound.

STEPS:

1. Acclimate your dog to the sound of the whistle.

2. Blow the whistle in a varying tone.

3. Immediately hold up a treat and excitedly call your dog.

4. Give your dog the treat.

Teach "Go Home"

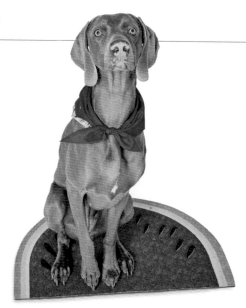

BEFORE YOU START

Set a cookie jar filled with treats in several rooms. This way you'll be able to quickly reward your dog any time you wish to.

TROUBLESHOOTING

MY DOG WON'T LEAVE MY SIDE.
Are you carrying the treats in your pocket? Have no treats on you; keep them all in the house in the cookie jar. Your dog will learn to "lead you" there.

TIP! You can use this same strategy to teach your dog to "go to the car."

TEACH IT:

"Go home" directs your dog to run to his house. This is useful when you are operating machinery and need your dog to clear out of the way, or if your dog strays out of bounds and a neighbor shouts it at him.

1 Start right at your front door. Point to the house, excitedly direct your dog to "go home," and immediately open the door and run inside with her.

2 Once inside, run to the cookie jar and give her a treat.

3 Now start from farther away. Point and tell your dog to "go home!"

4 Run all the way home with her, to the cookie jar.

5 Practice with a second person. One of you sends the dog, and the other waits at home with a treat.

WHAT TO EXPECT: Dogs learn to "go home" fairly easily. Using your pointed finger and excited tone will go a long way in giving her the right idea.

STEPS:

1 Say "go home!" and run inside with her.

2 Run to the cookie jar for a treat.

3 Start from farther away.

4 Again, run all the way home with her.

5 Practice with a second person: one to send the dog and one to welcome her home with a treat.

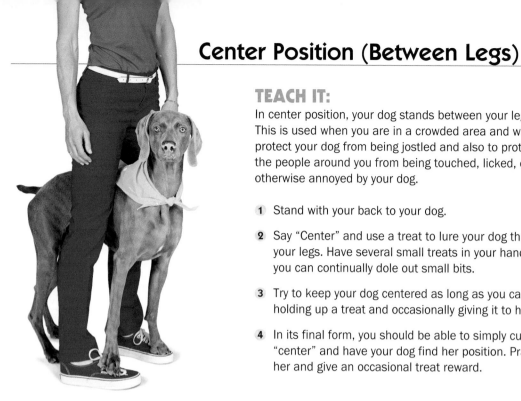

Center Position (Between Legs)

TEACH IT:

In center position, your dog stands between your legs. This is used when you are in a crowded area and wish to protect your dog from being jostled and also to protect the people around you from being touched, licked, or otherwise annoyed by your dog.

1 Stand with your back to your dog.

2 Say "Center" and use a treat to lure your dog through your legs. Have several small treats in your hand so you can continually dole out small bits.

3 Try to keep your dog centered as long as you can by holding up a treat and occasionally giving it to her.

4 In its final form, you should be able to simply cue "center" and have your dog find her position. Praise her and give an occasional treat reward.

WHAT TO EXPECT: Dogs love this exercise and after they learn it, will often center spontaneously just to be close to you.

BEFORE YOU START

Is your dog wary of standing under you? Practice permitting petting and affection (page 44).

TROUBLESHOOTING

I CAN'T GET MY DOG TO POSITION BEHIND ME.

It is much easier to move your body in front of your dog than to try to get your dog lined up behind you. Just keep rotating until your back is to your dog.

TIP! Give praise and a neck scratch in center position to make this a pleasant place to be.

STEPS:

1 Stand with your back to your dog.

2 Lure your dog through your legs.

3 Hold your dog at center by showing her a treat.

4 In its final form, simply cue your dog to "center."

Chapter 8

Appropriate Games to Play

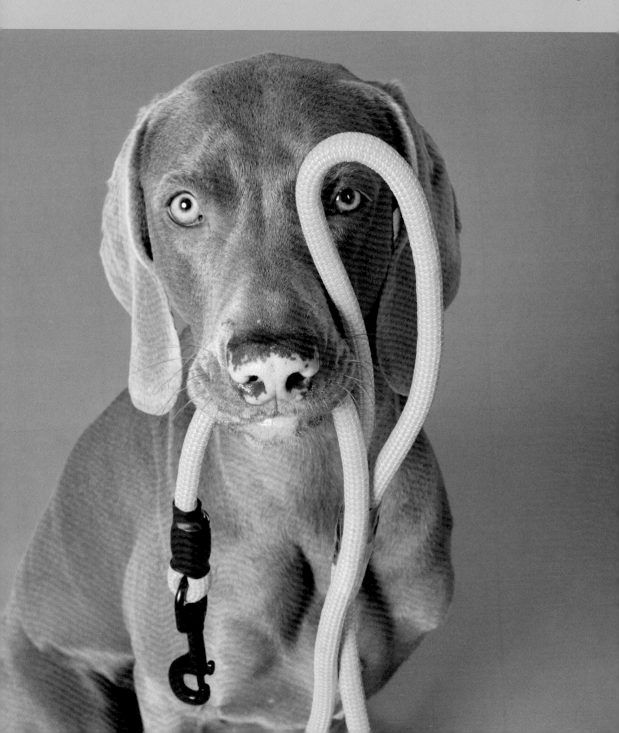

Romping

around with your dog is not only a fun part of dog ownership, but it's also a bonding experience and an opportunity to practice rules and boundaries within a defined structure.

Games are only fun if the game is challenging, the players are well-matched, and neither player is fearful or intimidated. Follow the tips in this chapter to give a pleasant gaming experience to both yourself and your dog.

You'll find that the benefits of playing appropriate games with your dog extend beyond the game session. It will increase your value in your dog's eyes, as you become a fun and exciting person that your dog instinctively gravitates to. When you call your dog, watch her come running!

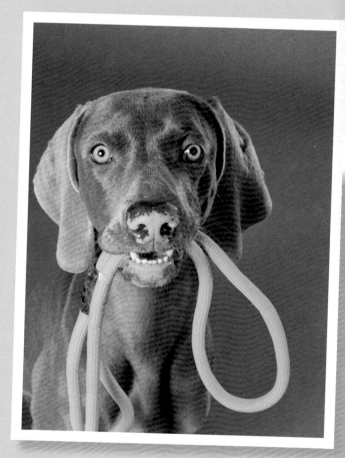

Tug

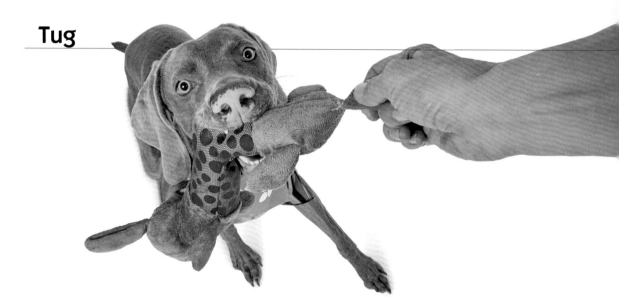

BEFORE YOU START

Choose a good tug toy: fluffy with fringes or hanging bits. A squeaker or squishy body helps.

TROUBLESHOOTING

MY DOG HAS NO INTEREST IN TUGGING.

Make your own tug toy with a mesh cloth and food (cheese, hot dogs) stuffed inside. Your dog will initially lick the toy and then bite down on it. With every bite or tug, a little food will squirt through the mesh.

TIP! Always let your dog win.

TEACH IT:

Many (but not all) dogs enjoy a game of tug as it indulges their instinctive drive. Introduce this game to your dog gently so as not to scare her off of it.

1. Engage your dog with the toy. Show it to her and hide it behind your back. Make it skittle away like a real, live prey animal.

2. Have it peek out from behind you, and when your dog goes for it have it run away. The toy should move AWAY from your dog, not toward her.

3. When she catches the toy, wiggle and tug it gently in a side to side (not front to back) motion.

4. After a few seconds let your dog pull it from your hands. This is her reward; the satisfaction of winning her prize. Praise her as she prances around with it.

WHAT TO EXPECT: Some breeds (such as terriers and herding breeds) have a much higher tug drive, but all dogs enjoy tugging to some extent. The more you play this game with your dog, the more her drive will develop.

STEPS:

1 Make the toy skittle away like a real prey animal.

2 The toy always runs AWAY from your dog.

3 When she catches it, wiggle it side to side.

4 Let her pull it from your hands as her reward.

Fetch

TEACH IT:

Is your dog uninterested in retrieving a ball? Or does he get the ball and then run off with it? We can fix that!

1. Use a box cutter to make a slit in a tennis ball.

2. Show your dog as you drop some treats inside.

3. Toss the ball and excitedly encourage your dog to get it. Your dog just saw the treats dropped inside and so will be interested in getting that ball.

4. Encourage your dog back to you by crouching and patting your legs. Your dog may want to keep this valuable food-ball for herself, so the first time may take a little effort to get her back, but keep at it.

5. When you get the ball back, squeeze it to make the treat drop out.

6. Let your dog eat the treats.

WHAT TO EXPECT: The first time getting the ball back will be the hardest, but very soon your dog will figure out that she can't get the treat out on her own and needs to bring it back to you to release the treat.

STEPS:

1. Make a slit in a tennis ball.

2. Drop some treats inside.

3. Toss the ball.

4. Encourage your dog back.

5. Squeeze the ball to release the treats.

6. Let her eat the treats.

Wrestling

TEACH IT:
Dogs can really enjoy wrestling, so long as it is gentle.

1. Cover and uncover your dog with a blanket. Or cover yourself with the blanket and call to your dog.

2. Goose her rear or nip playfully at her tail with your fingers.

3. Showing her belly can be a submissive gesture or an invitation to play. Stay to the side of your dog and avoid hovering over her.

4. Lift up her ears; pull them forward to cover her eyes.

WHAT TO EXPECT: Dogs wrestle in different ways, so it will be up to you to be observant and notice which games your dog likes and which she finds irritating or intimidating. As a rule of thumb, start small and gentle; ideally with just one finger.

STEPS:

1 Cover your dog or yourself with a blanket.

2 Nip playfully at her tail.

3 When your dog shows her belly, avoid hovering over her.

4 Lift her ears and cover her eyes.

Chase Me

TROUBLESHOOTING

MY DOG JUST STANDS THERE AND DOESN'T CHASE ME.

Take one of your dog's toys and hold it out behind you as you run. Or enlist another dog to chase you, to get your dog started. A treat in your hand can also do the trick.

TIP! The more excited you are, the more excited your dog will be.

TEACH IT:

Dogs have an instinctive chase drive and will enjoy a game of running after you.

1. Crouch lower and lower, and, in a suspenseful voice, start counting down ... "Ready, set, go!"

2. Take off running excitedly. Encourage your dog to chase you by calling to her and looking back over your shoulder.

3. Let your dog catch you and play with her when she does.

WHAT TO EXPECT: Some dogs simply adore this game. You may find that they even start picking up "naughty" items (such as your shoe) to goad you into a chase game.

STEPS:

1 Crouch down and say, "Ready, set, go!"

2 Take off running excitedly.

3 When your dog catches you, play with her.

Find Me (Learn My Name)

BEFORE YOU START

Enlist a family member or other person to help teach this skill.

TROUBLESHOOTING

MY DOG DOESN'T GET IT.

Start slower; just hide at the other end of the room behind a chair. Give treats when she finds you.

TIP! Use names in daily conversation with your dog; when your husband comes home from work, say, "Look, it's Randy!"

TEACH IT:

It's useful to have your dog know your name and the names of family members. You can then have your dog find a certain person.

1. Ask someone to hold your dog and then leave the room and hide in an obvious place.

2. Your helper should excitedly point to where you left and say, "Find [your name]!"

3. Your dog will search for you by scent. If she is having trouble finding you, help her by making little noises or poking your head a tiny bit into view. If she's still having trouble, call her name.

4. When your dog finds you, give her praise and petting and a treat. Reinforce the cue by saying, "Good find [your name]!"

WHAT TO EXPECT: This is a fun game for your dog! It engages his scent searching instinct and has a great reward of finding YOU at the end!

STEPS:

1 Have someone hold your dog while you go hide.

2 Your helper points and says, "Find [your name]!"

3 Your dog will search for you by scent.

4 Give a treat and reinforce the cue with "Good find [your name]!"

Make a Learning Challenge Toy

TROUBLESHOOTING

MY LITTLE DOG CAN'T GET HER LITTLE MOUTH AROUND THE BALL.
Some little dogs figure out how to roll the ball to cause the treat to flip out. Otherwise you can use a newspaper ball instead of a tennis ball.

TIP! Give your dog this challenge before dinner, to keep her entertained for five minutes while you prepare her food.

TEACH IT:

This DIY dog toy builds your dog's confidence, tenacity, and scenting ability. It will also get your dog out of your hair for five minutes!

1. Place a treat or kibble in each cup of a muffin tin.

2. Let your dog find all the treats.

3. Set it up again, but this time cover half of the treats with tennis balls.

4. Your dog will have to push, roll, or pick the tennis balls up to get at the treats. If she is having trouble, lift one of the balls to expose the treat and replace it. This should encourage your dog to keep searching!

5. If your dog is overly rambunctious, you may have to hold the tin down with your hand or foot.

WHAT TO EXPECT: Even rambunctious dogs tend to be calm and methodical with this challenge.

STEPS:

1 Place a treat or kibble in each cup of a muffin tin.

2 Let your dog find all the treats.

3 This time cover half of the treats with tennis balls.

4 If your dog has trouble getting the treats, lift a ball to show her where it is hiding.

5 Secure the muffin tin with your foot.

Chapter 9

Getting Braver:

Overcoming Common Fears

Courage can be learned. There are two science-based methods that we can use to gradually change our dogs' perception of a situation from one of fear to one of ambivilence or even excitement and joy. The steps in this chapter will walk you through the incremental process of overcoming your dog's fear.

Positive redirection is the distracting of your dog from the feared object by encouraging him into a more rewarding situation. Instead of leaving him to stress about being home alone, we give him a food toy to struggle with.

Counterconditioning is the process of exposing your dog to a low level of the feared object, and then pairing the onset of that object with yummy food. It's almost like the object predicts a yummy food treat.

Notice how one or both of these methods are being used in every skill in this chapter.

Increase Confidence with a Home-Base Pedestal

TEACH IT:

Pedestal training is a strategy used to increase confidence in dogs and puppies. Dogs are naturally height-seeking, and this advantage makes them feel more confident. A pedestal acts as a "home base" for your dog, giving him a default, secure place to be. Teach your dog to get on the pedestal.

1. Hold several treats at your dog's nose. Tell her "step up" and slowly move your hand up over the pedestal, luring her nose to follow it. Give her little treats along the way to keep her motivated but continue to lure her farther and farther onto the pedestal.

2. When your dog makes it all the way onto the pedestal, give her treats and praise and petting. Make the pedestal a super-rewarding place to be.

3. When your dog is on the pedestal, she is in an implied "stay." She should not be allowed to jump off of it at will; rather only when you ask her to. Say "Off" and pat your leg or the back of her neck to cue her dismount.

4. As she improves, see if you can send her to "step up" from farther away. Continue to use an arm sweep signal that is similar to the initial luring motion that she was taught with. Give a treat while she is on the pedestal.

WHAT TO EXPECT: If you make the pedestal a rewarding place to be (with treats and petting) your dog will take to it very quickly, and you'll likely find her jumping on her pedestal without having been asked!

BEFORE YOU START

A pedestal can be any raised object that is kind of small, such as an ottoman. A raised dog bed is generally too short to make a good pedestal.

TROUBLESHOOTING

WHAT ROOM SHOULD I PUT THE PEDESTAL IN?

It's handy to have a pedestal in every room. They need not all be identical.

TIP! Want to pet your dog? Ask her to go to her pedestal and pet her there.

STEPS:

1 Use several small treats to lure your dog onto the pedestal.

2 Give her treats and petting on top.

3 Cue "off" to dismount.

4 Send her to "step up" with an arm sweep.

Fear of an Object

BEFORE YOU START

It can sometimes help if you let your dog hang back while you go over to the feared object; touch it, move it, and show your dog how it works.

TROUBLESHOOTING

THE FEARED OBJECT MOVED / FELL ON MY DOG / STARTLED MY DOG AND NOW SHE IS MORE SCARED THAN EVER!

This can be a big setback. But there is one (and only one) way to get over that fear—with baby steps. It could take several weeks and a lot of patience, but eventually your dog will get there.

TIP! Your dog will gain confidence watching another dog approach the feared object.

TEACH IT:

For a dog to overcome his fear of an object, he must approach it on his own. Coax him to do so by playing the "bull's-eye game;" place treats closer and closer to the object.

1. Place a treat a far distance from the feared object. You want to get your dog excited about the game, so she needs to have zero fear when getting the first few treats.

2. Let your dog get the treat.

3. Continue to place treats closer and closer to the bull's-eye.

4. Your dog will cautiously take the treat and then most likely run back to you. Give her another treat when she does.

5. If at any time your dog stops progressing, regress back to an easier distance.

6. Step by step, your dog will gain confidence and conquer her fear.

WHAT TO EXPECT: The process of counter-conditioning (pairing a good thing with the feared thing) has many periods of regression. This step backward is usually only needed for a short while and will give them the momentum to push forward again.

STEPS:

1 Place a treat a far distance from the object.

2 Let your dog get the treat.

3 Place treats closer to the bull's-eye.

4 Give your dog a treat every time she successfully gets a treat from the ground.

5 If your dog stalls, regress back to an easier step.

6 With baby steps, your dog will conquer her fear!

Fear of Loud Sounds

TEACH IT:

Is your dog afraid of thunder, fireworks, and loud sounds? Use the process of counterconditioning to pair a yummy treat with the scary sound. Use the "bang game" to let your dog initiate the loud sound.

1. Hold the board down with your foot. Use a treat to lure your dog to step on the board.

2. When she does, let her have the treat.

3. Next time, hold the board an inch (2.5 cm) off the ground and lure her to step on it.

4. Let the board drop to the ground. The sound will startle her. The instant you hear the sound, pop a treat in her mouth.

5. Keep pairing the food reward with the bang sound, and eventually your dog will be banging with gusto!

WHAT TO EXPECT: Counterconditioning is the most effective method of reducing a fear. Don't rush progress, as you want to keep the sound below your dog's fear threshold.

BEFORE YOU START

Rig a board in a teeter-totter configuration.

TROUBLESHOOTING

IT BANGED ONCE, AND NOW MY DOG IS TOO AFRAID TO TRY IT AGAIN.

Lay the board flat on the floor. Put a towel on it to change the surface. Work your way back up to the teeter-totter.

TIP! Don't have a teeter-totter? You can play this game by banging a kitchen cabinet closed.

STEPS:

1 Use a treat to lure your dog onto the board.

2 When she does, give her the treat.

3 This time, hold the board an inch (2.5 cm) off the ground.

4 The instant the board drops and makes a sound, give her the treat.

5 Eventually your dog will be slamming that board!

Fear of Being Left Alone

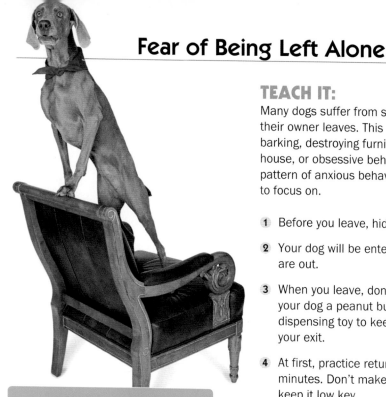

TEACH IT:

Many dogs suffer from separation anxiety when their owner leaves. This can manifest as whining and barking, destroying furniture, relieving themselves in the house, or obsessive behaviors. Help your dog break this pattern of anxious behavior by giving her something else to focus on.

1. Before you leave, hide treats all around the house.

2. Your dog will be entertained and distracted while you are out.

3. When you leave, don't make a big deal of it. Hand your dog a peanut butter-stuffed Kong or food-dispensing toy to keep her busy while you make your exit.

4. At first, practice returning home after just a few minutes. Don't make a big deal with your entrance; keep it low key.

WHAT TO EXPECT: Separation anxiety is a difficult condition to remedy. Improvements will be small and slow, but take comfort in knowing that with every small step, it WILL get better.

BEFORE YOU START

Dogs are extremely good associative learners; they know that when you pick up your keys you are about to leave. Keep your exiting ritual concise.

TROUBLESHOOTING

MY DOG IS SO ANXIOUS SHE IS HURTING HERSELF.

There are medications that your vet can prescribe to help with extreme anxiety.

TIP! Practice leaving and coming right back a few minutes later, so your dog realizes that not every time you leave is for a long time.

STEPS:

1 Hide treats around the house.

2 Your dog will be busy searching for treats.

3 Distract your dog with a peanut butter Kong while you make a subtle exit.

4 After a few minutes, return home. Keep it low-key.

Fear of Some People

BEFORE YOU START
Before introducing your dog to a "scary person," stand outside the supermarket and let your dog interact and receive treats from non-scary people, to develop a pattern.

TROUBLESHOOTING

MY DOG WON'T EVEN DO THE FIRST STEP.
That's all right, it takes time. Have the stranger offer the treat for a minute or two, and then move on to the next person. Keep your dog's mind moving.

TIP! Good treats make a world of difference. Try people food such as ham, steak, chicken, and cheese.

TEACH IT:
Dogs can have fears of different types of people, including fear of men, children, people in hats or hoods, people in uniform, people in wetsuits or snowsuits or dark clothes, etc. Help your dog overcome her fear by showing her that these people carry treats!

1   Hang out in front of the supermarket and recruit a person whom you think your dog will be afraid of. Give that person a handful of treats.

2   Have the stranger kneel down, turn away, and simply DROP a treat on the ground.

3   After a few successes, see if your dog will take a treat from his hand.

4   Have the stranger face your dog but not make eye contact as he offers more treats.

5   Stand up ... more treats.

6   By this time, your dog will be pretty pleased with her new buddy! Repeat this exercise a dozen times.

WHAT TO EXPECT: The more new people your dog is able to take treats from, the more rapidly his confidence with people will accelerate. Carry treats with you whenever you have your dog, so you can practice often.

STEPS:

1 Give a handful of yummy treats to a stranger.

2 Have him drop treats on the ground.

3 Can your dog take a treat from his hand?

4 The stranger should avoid eye contact.

5 Continue to give treats while standing a bit taller.

6 Your dog has a new buddy!

Fear of Other Dogs

BEFORE YOU START

If your dog is already apprehensive of new dogs, it is very important that you select dogs for him to interact with that are sure to be friendly.

TROUBLESHOOTING

EVER SINCE MY DOG WAS ATTACKED BY A DOG, HE IS SCARED OF DOGS.

Your dog needs to know that you will protect him; take on that role. If a dog comes running toward you, stand in front of your dog and yell "No!" to the oncoming dog. That show of strength will go a long way in your dog's eyes.

TIP! Never force your dog close to another dog. Always allow him an escape route.

TEACH IT:

When your dog sees another dog, does he tremble or hug against your leg? Does he snap at the other dog to scare him away? Help your dog make friends with these strategies.

1. Take both dogs on a walk. This will allow them to bond as a pack, without asking them to directly interact.

2. Sit between the two dogs and play with a squeak toy. This again will allow them to be in the same space but focused on something other than each other. It will also give your dog confidence to have you in control of the situation.

3. Present two biscuits to the dogs at the same time. This gives your dog a pleasant association between being near the new dog and getting a treat. Give the treats at the same time to avoid jealousy.

4. Is your dog nervous? Have him do a trick to get him to focus on you, while allowing him to be in the presence of the new dog.

WHAT TO EXPECT: The more successful encounters your dog has with new dogs, the easier it will be for him to make new friends.

STEPS:

1 Take both dogs on a walk.

2 Sit between them with a squeaky toy.

3 Present two biscuits at the same time.

4 Have your dog do tricks in the presence of the other dog.

Fear of Vacuum Cleaner

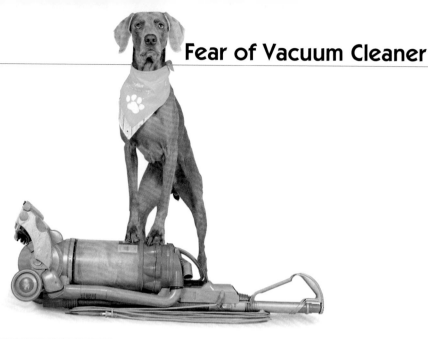

Don't startle your dog by turning on the vacuum cleaner while she is asleep. Make sure she has an escape route.

TROUBLESHOOTING

I DON'T THINK MY DOG IS AFRAID OF THE VACUUM CLEANER; I THINK SHE WANTS TO ATTACK IT!
Although her behavior looks aggressive, it actually stems from fear and anxiety. She is trying to frighten the machine away.

TIP! If your dog is afraid of the vacuum ... you're not cleaning enough!

TEACH IT:

Does just wheeling the vacuum cleaner out of the closet cause your dog to run for cover? Does she bark and snap at this monster? Help your dog make peace with this enemy.

1. Desensitize your dog to the vacuum cleaner; leave it in the room. Turn it on for a second and off again.

2. Vacuum with your back to your dog, pushing the vacuum cleaner away from—not toward—your dog.

3. Your dog will have more confidence if she is high up, on a chair.

4. Give your dog a peanut butter-filled Kong toy or a chew stick to work on while you vacuum. This will help acclimate her to being in the same room with the machine.

WHAT TO EXPECT: Dogs can absolutely become accustomed to the vacuum cleaner. By making the effort to get your dog used to it, you are helping her become a more confident dog with less general anxiety.

STEPS:

1 Turn the vacuum cleaner on and off again.

2 Push the vacuum cleaner AWAY from your dog.

3 Your dog will have more confidence if she is high up.

4 Give your dog a peanut butter-filled Kong or chew stick.

Fear of Slippery Floors

BEFORE YOU START
Leash your dog to control the situation. Never use the leash to pull your dog onto the floor.

TROUBLESHOOTING

IT'S NOT THAT MY DOG IS AFRAID; SHE LITERALLY HAS TROUBLE WALKING ON THE FLOOR.
Make sure her nails are trimmed (page 46). There are extended-wear adhesive paw stickers and rubber nail covers to help with traction.

TIP! All dogs are apprehensive about walking on a shiny black floor, such as black marble. It appears to them to be basically a black hole.

TEACH IT:

Is your dog afraid to walk through the kitchen? Up the stairs? Across the linoleum floor at the vet's office? Help her overcome this fear of slippery floors.

1. Put a treat in a dog bowl (as it is large and visual) at the edge of the slippery floor. Let your dog go get it.

2. Use bath mats to make a pathway to the food bowl. Walk next to your dog as she makes the journey.

3. Start to add some gaps between the bath mats that your dog will have to navigate over.

4. Enthusiastic praise will go a long way in encouraging your dog.

WHAT TO EXPECT: Using this method, dogs can usually start walking on a slippery floor within a day or two.

STEPS:

1. Put a treat in a bowl at the edge of the floor. Let your dog get it.

2. Make a walkway of bath mats to the bowl.

3. Start to separate the bath mats.

4. Lots of praise will accelerate the process.

Fear of Bathtub

BEFORE YOU START

Take a moment to prepare. Close the door so your wet dog can't run amok. Have your towels, brush, and shampoo all within reach, and have your treat bag open so you can access it with one hand.

TROUBLESHOOTING

MY DOG SNARLS AT ME!

Don't make this into a fight, but don't end the bath when your dog snarls or he will learn that he can always end a bath by snarling. Instead, simply go as far as you can. If that means he sits in a dry tub for 5 minutes, then do that. Next time you'll get a litter farther.

TIP! Smear some peanut butter on the side of the tub and let your dog lick it while you bathe him.

TEACH IT:

Does your dog cower when you say the word "bath"? Does he freeze up when his nails hit the porcelain of the tub? Make bathtime easier with these simple steps.

1. Place a towel in the empty, dry tub to give your dog secure footing. Toss a treat in there, and encourage him to jump in after it. Repeat this several times.

2. Run a trickle of water with the drain open.

3. Gradually let the water level rise with your dog in the tub. Distract him with sudsing up.

4. Giving treats during the bath never hurts. Some dogs will be too anxious to eat the treats, which is normal.

WHAT TO EXPECT: Few dogs ever really LIKE baths, but by approaching it in a gentle, slow manner we can avoid a chaotic scene and get through the chore smoothly.

STEPS:

1. Place a towel in the dry tub. Encourage your dog to get the treats.

2. Run a trickle of water with the drain open.

3. Let the water level rise as you suds him up.

4. Offer your dog treats (although he may not take them).

Chapter 10

Troubleshoot the Most

Common Behavior Problems

Unruly behavior can cause havoc in your household. It can be annoying, chaotic, embarrassing, and dangerous to your dog or to other people. This chapter addresses each of the most common behavior problems with step-by-step responses.

Some of these problems do not have easy solutions. Continually barking or urine marking in your house are instinctual behaviors that will be very difficult to extinguish. In those cases, the advice in this chapter will lean toward realistic information and ways to manage the behavior you cannot change.

Patience and the ability to keep control of your own frustration are the most important qualities in a successful trainer.

Jumping on Visitors

BEFORE YOU START

Teach your dog to wait on a pedestal (page 110).

TROUBLESHOOTING

THIS WORKS IN PRACTICE, BUT WHEN AN ACTUAL VISITOR COMES IT ALL TURNS TO CHAOS.

It's not easy. Call through the door that you are preparing the dog and need a minute. As you open the door, never take your eyes off of your dog. You are a dog trainer; act like one.

TIP! This method also works well to control the greeting when you return from work. As you walk in the door, send your dog to her pedestal and greet her there.

TEACH IT:

Does your dog jump up on visitors? Teach her to wait politely on her pedestal and allow the visitor to approach her on THEIR terms. Practice this strategy over and over with a friend.

1   Ring the doorbell, send your dog to the pedestal (page 110), and give her a treat. You want the sound of the doorbell to eventually be a cue for her to get on the pedestal.

2   While she is on the pedestal, practice opening and closing the door. Give her a treat while she is standing on the pedestal.

3   Now practice with a friend.

4   If your dog jumps off the pedestal to greet the visitor, the visitor should turn his back and ignore your dog. Your dog won't like to be ignored and will learn to stay on her pedestal to get attention.

5   If your dog stays on her pedestal, allow the visitor to approach her and give her a treat.

WHAT TO EXPECT: Dogs actually enjoy a pedestal greeting as it allows them to be up high, where they can better see and interact with the visitor.

STEPS:

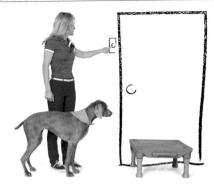 

1 Teach your dog that the doorbell means she should run to her pedestal.

2 Practice opening and closing the door.

3 Now practice with a friend.

4 If your dog jumps off, your visitor should ignore her.

5 Polite dogs get dog biscuits!

Dashing Out the Door

TEACH IT:

When you open the front door, does your dog bolt outside? Here are some techniques to gain control.

SCENARIO #1: DOG ON LEASH

1. Use this technique when you and your dog are exiting together. Send your dog to her pedestal (page 110).

2. Attach her leash while she is on the pedestal. The confined space will keep things calm.

3. You lead the way, exiting the door first.

SCENARIO #2: YOU LEAVE WITHOUT THE DOG

1. Use this technique when you are leaving for work. Send your dog to her pedestal (page 110) and leave.

2. When you come back, send your dog to her pedestal.

3. Only when she is on her pedestal do you give her attention and treats.

WHAT TO EXPECT: A pedestal is invaluable in controlling door dashing. It will take a few extra seconds, but make sure your dog is on the pedestal every time before you open the door.

BEFORE YOU START
Teach your dog to wait on a pedestal (page 110).

TROUBLESHOOTING

I HAVE SEVERAL DOGS.
You can absolutely use this method with several dogs. Have a pedestal for each. Require all dogs to stay on the pedestals before any of them get a treat.

TIP! Treats only happen on the pedestal.

STEPS:

SCENARIO #1: DOG ON LEASH

1 Send your dog to her pedestal.

2 Attach her leash in this confined space.

3 Lead the way as you exit.

SCENARIO #2: YOU LEAVE WITHOUT THE DOG

1 Send your dog to her pedestal and leave.

2 When you come home, send her to her pedestal.

3 Only then does she get attention.

Begging at the Table

BEFORE YOU START

Teach your dog spot training (page 74).

TROUBLESHOOTING

DO I HAVE TO GIVE TREATS FOREVER?

It will be most effective if you continue to give at least a few treats during your meal, forever.

TIP! Treats only happen on the dog bed.

TEACH IT:

Does your dog pace, whine, and paw at you at the dinner table? Use these steps to easily train her to lie down.

1 Have your dog lie down on her dog bed (page 74) next to the table.

2 Have a treat jar on the table. Every few minutes, give your dog a treat.

3 If your dog wanders around, send her back to her spot.

4 You'll be surprised at how long your dog will hold her position in hopes of another treat!

WHAT TO EXPECT: This method is very effective and takes the stress out of dinnertime begging (for merely the cost of a few treats). Your dog is practicing self-control, and rehearsing the behavior of lying down politely.

STEPS:

1 Set your dog's bed next to the table.

2 Every few minutes, give her a treat.

3 If she wanders, send her back to her spot.

4 She will learn to wait a long time for her next treat.

Chewing Shoes / Furniture

TEACH IT:

Some dogs (especially puppies) will chew destructively on your shoes, furniture, or other inappropriate items. Use these simple steps to manage this behavior problem.

1. Don't set your dog up for failure by leaving your shoes out and then punishing her for chewing them. Put your shoes away.

2. If your dog has your shoe, do not chase her (as she thinks this is a fun game). Tell her "No, drop it" (page 60).

3. Replace the shoe with something better, such as a chew toy. Say "good" when you give it to her.

4. Your dog wants to chew, so give her something appropriate to chew on. Provide a variety of rubber and rawhide chews.

5. To deter your dog from chewing on furniture, rub wintergreen oil on it. This is an essential oil with a strong, refreshing odor that deters dogs. It is organic with no dangerous chemicals.

WHAT TO EXPECT: Dogs chew for two reasons: for fun or from anxiety. Young dogs chew for fun and start to outgrow it as they get older. In either case, providing chew toys will go a long way to reducing the problem.

BEFORE YOU START
Teach your dog to drop it (page 60).

TROUBLESHOOTING
MY DOG EATS (AND SWALLOWS) WEIRD ITEMS.
The abnormal habit of ingesting non-nutritive items like dirt, sand, clay, paper, chalk, fabric, or plastic is referred to as *pica*. The best way to prevent your dog from ingesting these things is to limit his access to them.

TIP! If you don't want your dog to chew on your new shoes, then don't give her old shoes as a chew toy.

STEPS:

1. Set your dog up for success. Put your shoes away.

2. Tell her "No, drop it."

3. Replace the shoe with a chew toy.

4. Provide a variety of rubber and rawhide chews.

5. Rub wintergreen oil on the furniture.

Digging

TROUBLESHOOTING

WHY DO DOGS DIG?

Dogs dig for several reasons: to make a cool hole to lie in, as an instinct to make a den, to bury a bone, to hunt a gopher, to escape the yard, from separation anxiety, or simply for entertainment. Figuring out why your dog is digging is the first step to providing a solution.

TIP! Some breeds, like terriers, are more likely to dig than others.

TEACH IT:

Is your dog digging up your yard? Some dogs want to dig, and it is futile to try to stop this behavior entirely. Instead, try one of these tactics to give your dog an appropriate place to expend her energy.

1. Dogs sometimes dig to find a cool spot to lie in. Define an area where she is allowed to dig, and add water to make it extra appealing to dig in.

2. To avoid muddy paws, make a digging spot filled with wood shavings or rubber mulch.

3. Section off a part of your lawn with shade and lush green grass or sand, both of which are ideal for digging.

4. An elevated dog bed will keep your dog cooler than a bed on the ground. This cool spot may stop your dog's desire to cool off by digging a hole.

WHAT TO EXPECT: Giving your dog an appropriate place to dig is an effective way to get her to stop digging up your yard.

STEPS:

1 Water down an area that is appropriate for your dog to dig in.

2 Wood shavings or rubber mulch make a clean digging spot.

3 Section off a grass digging spot.

4 An elevated bed may stop your dog's desire to cool off by digging.

Going into the Trash Can

BEFORE YOU START
The easiest solution is to simply buy a better trash can. Problem solved; no battles.

TROUBLESHOOTING

MY DOG HAS FIGURED OUT HOW TO OPEN THE TRASH CAN LID!
Dogs are smart! Some figure out how to operate a step can, unhinge a locking lid, or push the can over to release its contents. A heavy-duty, well-made trash can will decrease stress in your household.

TIP! Look for "pet-proof" trash cans which have locking lids.

TEACH IT:
Do you come home to find trash strewn about the house? Teach your dog to stay out of the trash can.

1. Put a few pennies in an empty soda can.

2. Sneak up on your dog when she has her head buried in the trash can ...

3. ... and shake the shaker-can! This should startle your dog and cause her to pull her head out of the trash can.

4. Act like you don't know where that sound came from; "What happened?" You want your dog to think that her going in the trash can caused this startling sound.

5. Use positive redirection; send your dog to her pedestal (page 110) and reward her there with a treat or petting.

WHAT TO EXPECT: Results will vary depending on how sound-shy your dog is. Some dogs (such as gun-dog breeds) may not startle at all from the sound.

STEPS:

1 Put a few pennies in an empty soda can.

2 Sneak up on your dog when she has her head buried in the trash can ...

3 ... and shake the shaker-can!

4 "What happened?" Act like you don't know where that sound came from.

5 Send your dog to her pedestal for a positive reward.

Hyperactivity

BEFORE YOU START
Practice focus (page 50) to
teach your dog to give you calm
eye contact.

TROUBLESHOOTING

MY DOG IS HYPER ALL THE TIME!
You can't change a dog's
personality. Our goal is to
be able to get small bits of
calmness when we ask for it.

TIP! This "least reinforcing
scenario" method is also used to
teach safety to kids when around
hyper dogs (page 34).

TEACH IT:

When a dog is hyper, any attention (whether good or bad)
can reinforce or escalate the behavior. Therefore, when
a dog is overly excited, we use the "least reinforcing
scenario" to calm the situation.

1. When you play with your dog, there may come a time
   when she is too hyper, and you wish to de-escalate
   the situation.

2. Stop the game, turn your back on your dog, and
   ignore her.

3. Your dog will be a little unsure of what to do and will
   soon calm down and look at you.

4. Once she gives you calm attention, the game can
   resume. The game is her reward for the calm
   attention.

WHAT TO EXPECT: Every time your dog is too hyper,
remove your attention. And every time she gives you
calm eye contact, reward her with your attention. With
every repetition, your dog will learn this game and will be
quicker to give you her calm eye contact.

STEPS:

1 When your dog is too hyper, you may wish to de-escalate the situation.

2 Turn your back on your dog and remove your attention.

3 Your dog will soon calm down and look at you.

4 Once she gives you calm attention, the game can resume.

Barking

TEACH IT:

If your dog barks while you are not home, there is not a lot you can do other than control the environment (such as closing the blinds so your dog can't see out the windows). This page deals with the problem of your dog barking excessively while you are home. There are different reasons why your dog may be barking; address each one with its proper technique.

1. Barking because she wants to go outside: Install some doggy doorbells and teach her to use them to alert you (page 70).

2. Alert barking: If she sees something novel outside (a strange car or a squirrel) she may be trying to alert you. Go look, and assure her "It's nothing, settle down."

3. Barking for attention: Don't let your dog get in the habit of demanding attention from you by repeatedly barking at you. When she does this, REMOVE your attention.

4. Barking to scare away people: As much as it is in your control, do not allow this to be an effective technique. Instead, engage your dog when she turns her attention back to you.

5. Having your dog lie down (page 54) should cause her to stop barking.

WHAT TO EXPECT: Some types of barking are easier than others to stop. Excitable barking will be very difficult to change unless you are incredibly consistent with your training.

BEFORE YOU START

Choose a cue word for your dog to stop barking, such as "quiet!"

TROUBLESHOOTING

I HAVE SEVERAL DOGS AND ONCE ONE STARTS BARKING, THEY ALL BARK!

Dogs will definitely take cues from each other to join in the bark fest. Observe which one seems to initiate the barking and focus your training on that dog.

TIP! Some of the barkiest dog breeds are Chihuahua, dachshund, German shepherd, beagle, Yorkshire terrier, miniature schnauzer, West Highland white terrier, fox terrier, and Siberian husky.

STEPS:

1 Barking to go outside: Doggy doorbells.

2 Alert barking: Go look.

3 Barking for attention: Remove your attention when she barks.

4 Barking to scare away people: Engage her when she looks at you.

5 Lying down should stop the barking.

Troubleshoot the Most Common Behavior Problems

Puppy Biting, Nipping

BEFORE YOU START
Give your puppy chew toys and appropriate things to gnaw on.

TROUBLESHOOTING

MY ADULT DOG SOMETIMES NIPS MY ELBOWS OR NIPS MY FINGERS WHEN I FEED HER.
Use the same technique with an older dog. Say, "Ouch! That hurt! I'm not playing anymore," and walk away or stop giving food. They'll learn.

TIP! Puppies lose their baby teeth. Keep an eye out for those momentos!

TEACH IT:

As puppies' baby teeth grow in, they have the urge to bite on things, including your finger, nose, and ear. We gently inform the puppy (without punishment) that we don't like this behavior.

1 Puppies have control over how hard they bite. YOU decide what is an acceptable pressure.

2 If your puppy bites too hard, say, "Ouch! That hurt! I'm not playing with you anymore," and turn your back on your puppy.

3 After about 10 seconds, go back to playing with your puppy. Keep repeating this process.

WHAT TO EXPECT: Your puppy values your attention and engagement. Your puppy will learn that every time he bites too hard, he loses you. He will learn to not bite hard.

STEPS:

1 YOU decide how hard your puppy is allowed to bite.

2 Say, "Ouch! That hurt! I'm not playing with you anymore."

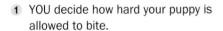

3 After 10 seconds, go back to playing with your puppy.

Peeing: Submissive or Excited

TEACH IT:

Is your dog housetrained ... until a visitor reaches for him? Does he immediately squat to pee in excitement or roll onto his back and pee from submissive fear? Manage this issue with these simple steps.

1. Potty your dog often to help her be successful. Clean and deodorize accidents when they do happen.

2. Visitors should approach your dog sideways, and not face forward as this could be intimidating and cause submissive peeing.

3. Visitors should get down low when they approach your dog.

4. Allow the dog to have an escape route. Don't let her feel boxed in.

5. Don't reach for the dog or hover over the dog.

6. Don't look directly at the dog, as this could be intimidating for her.

WHAT TO EXPECT: This behavioral problem can absolutely be fixed. The more successful experiences your dog has, where she meets people without peeing, the faster her learning will progress. Don't push too fast ... focus on successful experiences.

BEFORE YOU START

Enlist some friends to help you. Brief them beforehand on the steps shown here.

TROUBLESHOOTING

I'VE FOLLOWED ALL THE STEPS SHOWN HERE, BUT MY DOG IS STILL PEEING.

You need to work below her threshold. Observe where the line is that causes her to pee and stop before that line. That may mean your visitor sits in a chair clear across the room.

TIP! Men trigger submissive peeing in dogs more than women do.

STEPS:

1 Potty your dog often and clean up accidents.

2 Approach the dog sideways, not face-on.

3 Get down low when approaching the dog.

4 Make sure the dog has an escape route.

5 Don't reach over the dog.

6 Don't look directly at the dog.

Peeing: Marking Behavior

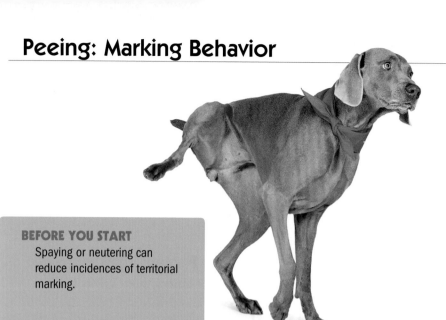

BEFORE YOU START
Spaying or neutering can reduce incidences of territorial marking.

TROUBLESHOOTING

IS MY NEW BOYFRIEND THE CAUSE OF MY DOG'S MARKING?
Your dog may start marking things around the house because someone new has been introduced into the household, whether it's a new roommate, pet, or frequent visitor. Allow your dog to spend some time bonding with the new person.

TIP! Punishment after the fact is ineffective and would lead only to confusion and possibly fear.

TEACH IT:
Territorial urine marking is a difficult behavior to extinguish. Below are some techniques you can use to reduce this problem behavior.

1. Clean soiled areas thoroughly with a cleaner specifically designed to eliminate urine odor, as dogs will re-mark those areas. Make previously soiled areas inaccessible, or else feed and play with your dog in the areas where he marks.

2. Watch your dog; when he begins to urinate, interrupt him with a loud noise and take him outside.

3. Put away items likely to cause marking, such as guests' belongings and new purchases.

WHAT TO EXPECT: If your dog has been marking for a long time, a pattern has already been established which will be difficult to break, even with spaying or neutering. Multiple dog households, particularly those with more than one male dog, may find this behavior even more prevalent and difficult to prevent.

STEPS:

1. Clean soiled areas. Make those areas inaccessible, or feed and play in those areas with your dog.

2. When he begins to urinate, interrupt him with a loud noise and take him outside.

3. Put away items likely to cause marking, such as guests' belongings and new purchases.

Humping

TEACH IT:

Humping is a behavior male dogs do when they mate. But dogs may hump other things and for other reasons. They mount furniture, stuffed toys, and people. Dogs may hump when they are excited, and it is common in puppies.

1. When a dog is humping a person, the person should just get up and walk away, which teaches the dog that this is an unacceptable behavior.

2. Some dogs hump as a dominance behavior. Tell your dog "no."

3. The best way to handle humping is with positive redirection. Distract the dog with a game or by asking for a trick.

4. This gives the dog a chance to be a "good dog" and receive the attention he is wanting.

WHAT TO EXPECT: Puppies and dogs outgrow this behavior as they age. It may still be common to see a brief bout of humping when the dog is playful and excited.

STEPS:

1. When a dog is humping a person, the person should just get up and walk away.

2. Some dogs hump as a dominance behavior. Tell your dog "no."

3. Use positive redirection. Distract the dog by asking for a trick.

4. This gives the dog a chance to be a "good dog" and receive the attention he is wanting.

Growling at You

TEACH IT:
Here are some steps to managing common growling situations.

1. Food bowl growling: Occasionally, while your dog is eating, walk over and drop a treat in his bowl. He'll learn you are not trying to take food from him. Alternately, toss a treat away from the bowl.

2. Growling on the bed or under the bed: Don't make this a battle. Simply lure your dog off or out with a treat. You are patterning her to obey, whether she realizes it or not. Do not give her the treat; ask her for a sit or other behavior, and then reward that good behavior.

3. Growling to protect a toy or bone: Have a better toy to trade for it.

WHAT TO EXPECT: We don't want to get bitten, but we also don't want to reward our dog for growling. So instead, we use positive redirection. We get our dog out of the growling situation, ask her for an alternate behavior, and then reward that good behavior.

STEPS:

1 Food bowl growling: While your dog is eating, drop a treat in his bowl. Alternately, toss a treat away from the bowl.

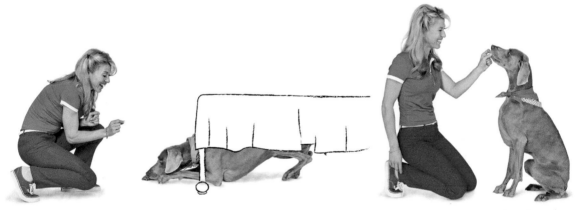

2 Growling on the bed or under the bed: Lure your dog off or out with a treat, but don't give it to her. Instead, ask for a sit and then give her the treat.

3 Growling to protect a toy or bone: Have a better toy to trade for it.

Aggression (Muzzle Training)

BEFORE YOU START

Basket muzzles (shown here) are the safest, allowing the dog to pant and drink.

TROUBLESHOOTING

MY DOG SHAKES HER HEAD AND PAWS AT THE MUZZLE.

It's new, and this is normal, but you want to interrupt it before it becomes a habit. Take her on a walk to get her mind on something else.

TIP! Put a pink bandana on your dog to make her look more friendly while she's wearing her muzzle.

TEACH IT:

Muzzles no longer have the negative connotation of the past. Nowadays, muzzles are recognized as a humane way of allowing your dog the freedom to be in public without the danger of aggression toward another dog or person. It is the correct, responsible thing to do—both for your dog and for the public. Never force the muzzle on your dog. Instead, train her to put it on willingly using these steps.

1. First introduce the muzzle to your dog with some yummy peanut butter.

2. Dab peanut butter on the inside of the muzzle. Allow your dog to put her snout in and lick it. You can also feed her treats through the front of the muzzle.

3. Once she is comfortable with that, buckle the strap behind her head.

4. She will want to fuss with the muzzle, so immediately take her on a walk to distract her.

WHAT TO EXPECT: When paired with positive experiences such as treats or walks, dogs take to muzzles quite readily. You'll most likely find that your dog will receive more walks and outings with you, now that you are relieved of the apprehension of a potential biting situation.

STEPS:

1 Introduce the muzzle with some peanut butter.

2 Dab peanut butter inside the muzzle or feed her treats through the front.

3 Buckle the strap behind her head.

4 Immediately take her on a walk to distract her.

Lunging at Bikes, etc.

TEACH IT:

Does your dog bark and lunge at passing bikes, skateboards, motorcycles, and cars? The more you allow your dog to engage in this predatory behavior, the worse it will become; interrupt the behavior with these steps.

1. Create distance by moving away from the vehicle.

2. Get your dog used to the object by having it be still and then gradually moving it back and forth. Your goal is to get your dog bored with it.

3. Redirect your dog; when she starts to focus in on the vehicle, get her attention by having her do a trick or giving her treats or doing something fun. Ideally, you want to pattern her so that every time she sees a bicycle, she whips her head around to look at you instead.

WHAT TO EXPECT: Instinctual drives, such as a chase drive, are always difficult to control. These three exercises are the best ways to eventually reduce the drive, although it may take several months to see a change.

STEPS:

1. Create distance by moving away from the vehicle.

2. Move the object back and forth until your dog gets bored with it.

3. Redirect your dog with a treat or by doing something fun.

Safely Break up a Dog Fight

TEACH IT:
Hopefully you'll never have to break up a dog fight, but it's important to be prepared to do it safely.

1. Recognize a potential dog fight before it starts and prevent it from escalating by clapping your hands or spraying the dog's nose with a water spray bottle.

2. If the dogs are engaged in a fight, pour a bucket of water on them.

3. If the dogs are locked on, you'll have to pull them apart. Identify the aggressor (the dog whose mouth is locked onto the other dog). Use your foot to sweep his back leg to test his reaction. He probably won't react, but it's safer to risk his biting your shoe than your hand.

4. Lift his back legs off the ground. This will remove his leverage, so he won't have tearing force on the other dog. Pull back slightly so that when the dog finally releases his jaws, he'll be pulled away from the fight.

5. When the dog releases his jaws, walk backward, pulling him with you. In extreme cases, the dog will redirect his aggression onto you. Avoid this situation by continuing to walk backward so he is unable to get his head to you. You can also spin in place, so that centrifical force keeps the dog's head spinning away from you.

WHAT TO EXPECT: This method of lifting the dog's rear legs is effective. Don't be in a rush, as the dog will be much less harmful to the other dog once he is in this lifted position. Once the dogs are separated, be aware that they may immediately try to engage again, so keep them separated.

STEPS:

1 Prevent a fight before it starts by clapping and using a spray bottle.

2 A bucket of water often breaks up small fights.

3 Identify the aggressor. Test his reaction to your foot sweep.

4 Lift his back legs and pull slightly backward.

5 When he releases, walk him backward.

Chapter 11

Good to Know

Awareness of common dog predicaments

ahead of time will save you angst in the moment when your dog starts chattering her teeth, sucking in air through her nose in long snorts, or emitting a noxious smell from her glands when frightened.

The lists in this chapter have been compiled with the contributions of veterinary professionals as well as new and long-time dog owners. Let their experience save you some uneccessary middle-of-the-night trips to the vet.

And, more importantly, the safety information contained in this chapter on poisonous substances and performing the Heimlich maneuver on a choking dog can save your dog's life.

Heimlich for Dogs (Choking)

PERFORM THE HEIMLICH MANEUVER IF YOUR DOG IS CHOKING

Most dogs will chew nearly anything: bones, toys, shoes, socks, etc. But would you know what to do if something became lodged in the windpipe or stuck on the palate and your dog began to choke?

If a dog is suffocating, he will often panic. A dog may paw at his mouth if something is lodged.

STEPS:

1 Lift the dog up off the ground like a wheel-barrow, with her head facing down. Try to shake the object out of her mouth using gravity.

2 Sweep from side to side to dislodge the object.

3 Use back blows. Forcefully strike five times between her shoulder blades with the heel of your hand.

4 Place your arms around her waist. Form a fist and cover the fist with your other hand. Place your fist on the soft spot just under the ribcage. Quickly and firmly give three to five thrusts inwards and upwards. Repeat three to five thrusts up to four times. Do not use excessive force.

Weird Things Dogs Do...

Reverse sneezing

Occurs more in brachycephalic (short-nosed) dogs. The dog makes rapid and long inhalations, stands still, and extends his head and neck. A loud snorting sound is produced.

Chattering teeth

A lump located on the roof of your dog's mouth, behind his front teeth, is called the Jacobson's Organ. It is receptive to pheromones (body scents or chemicals we emit in response to our emotional state). Dogs use this organ to gather information about other dogs and to "smell fear." Dogs access the organ by licking or snapping the air or chattering their teeth. You may see this after they smell or lick urine.

Express anal glands

Anal glands produce a foul-smelling, greasy substance that probably serves as a territorial marker and relays biochemical information. They occasionally become impacted or infected, and some vets and groomers express them manually (although the preferred solution is to switch the dog to a grain-free dog food).

Flea biting / corn cob nibbling

Sometimes called "corn cob nibbling" or "flea biting," this gentle nibble on your arm or shirt or loose thread on your clothes is an affectionate, self-soothing behavior done by some dogs. There is no need to curb this behavior unless you do not like it.

Nooking / suckling on stuffies

This hereditary trait is a self-soothing behavior where the dog suckles on a stuffie or blanket. There is no need to curb this behavior.

Fast panting

Dogs do not sweat through their skin, but they do sweat through their paw pads. They also cool themselves by panting. Panting may be with their mouth wide open and tounge hanging out, or it may be with mouth closed and very fast, short breaths.

...That are Actually Perfectly Normal

Eating feces

Coprophagia is common in dogs and may stem from a mother's instinct to clean the den of her puppies' feces. There are products which can be fed to the dog to give his feces a foul taste, however these products have limited success.

Growl-howl / growl-purr

Not all growls are aggressive. Some vocalizations may sound like a purring or howling growl and stem from excitement or pleasure. Some breeds (basenjis) even make a yodeling sound.

Hiccuping

Hiccuping is common in puppies and is usually attributed to an overindulgence of life: breathing, swallowing, running, etc.

Eating grass and throwing up

Dogs eat grass to cause themselves to vomit or because they need fiber. In either case, it is not desirable, as vomiting is a violent act that can irritate their bodies and result in a loss of electrolytes.

Humping dogs and people

Humping is more common in puppies and intact male dogs, but can be present in females as well. See pages 152 to 153 for more.

Zoomies

This is the term for those wild-eyed crazy circles younger dogs run when they get excited.

Belly scratch leg wave

Scratch the right spot on your dog's belly or side and his hind leg will reflexively mimic your scratching motion.

- The entire spoon when giving a pill with peanut butter
- Gravel under an outdoor grill, upon which grease has leaked
- An entire rawhide bone, in one piece
- Fish hooks at a beach or river (which had bits of fish stuck to them)
- Zipper-lock baggies that contain food (the zipper strip can clog their intestines)
- Towels
- Squeakers from toys
- Disposable razors
- Children's toys
- Batteries, watch batteries
- Tennis balls
- Chewing gum (the sweetener xylitol is extremely poisonous)
- Cigarette butts
- Soap bars
- Drywall
- Cooked bones
- Corn cobs (which can get stuck in their intestines)
- Sticks (often get stuck in their mouths)
- Feces in litterboxes
- Peach stones / pits
- Underwear
- Socks
- Diapers
- Pacifiers
- Condoms
- Feminine hygiene products
- Mouth retainers, dentures, hearing aids, ear plugs
- Hair scrunchies

Top 10 Toxins to Dogs

1. **Dark chocolate**

2. **Rodenticides / insecticides:**
   Including DEET pest repellent

3. **Xylitol:**
   A very toxic sweetener contained in many products, including sugar-free gum, some brands of peanut butter, and toothpaste

4. **NSAIDs (ibuprofen, naproxen, etc.):**
   May result in vomiting, ulcers, and kidney failure

5. **Grapes and raisins:**
   Can cause kidney failure

6. **Household cleaners:**
   Concentrated products such as toilet bowl, oven, and drain cleaners may cause chemical burns if licked.

7. **Acetaminophen (Tylenol):**
   The effects of acetaminophen poisoning are quite serious, often causing non-repairable liver damage.

8. **Fertilizers:**
   Be cautious of dogs walking on fertilized grass and then licking their paws.

9. **Mushrooms:**
   Poisonous mushrooms found growing in the yard can be extremely toxic, causing death.

10. **Corn on the cob:**
    May cause intestinal blockage

A Few More Poisonous Substances

- **Antifreeze:**
  Tastes good to dogs and is very toxic

- **Gorilla Glue:**
  Tastes good to dogs and will harden into a lump in their intestines

- **Raw / undercooked meat, eggs, and bones:**
  Can contain Salmonella and E. coli bacteria. Raw eggs decrease the absorption of biotin (a B vitamin), leading to skin and coat problems.

- **Yeast dough:**
  Can rise and cause gas in your dog's digestive system, causing the stomach to bloat and twist, becoming a life-threatening emergency.

- **Hops (used in home beer brewing):**
  Can be highly toxic. Death can occur in as little as six hours after ingestion.

- **Onions, garlic, chives:**
  In large amounts, can cause gastrointestinal irritation and red blood cell damage

- **Coconut water:**
  Is high in potassium and should not be given to your dog

- **Macadamia nuts:**
  Can cause vomiting

- **Milk and dairy:**
  Can cause diarrhea

- **Nuts (including almonds, pecans, and walnuts):**
  High in oils and fats, which can cause pancreatitis in large amounts

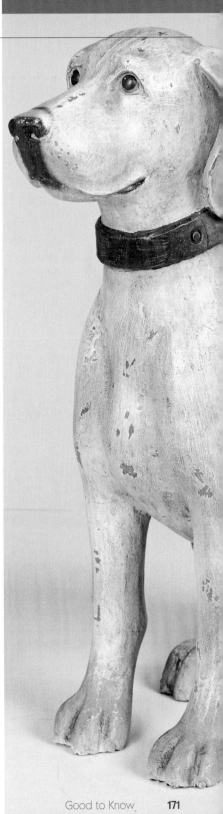

INDEX

ACKNOWLEDGMENTS

MODELS—Thanks to our beautiful, talented, and incredibly patient dogs: **Kimba** (Weimaraner with pink nose), **Jadie** (Weimaraner), **Bonny** (Shih Tzu), **Penny** (Chihuahua), **Rusty** (golden retreiver); and to our professional cat: **Neil** (Persian cat). Thanks to our adorable child model: **Melody Rischar**; and to our extra handsome male model and rockstar: **Randy Banis** (Kyra's husband).

Photographer: **Christian Arias** (Slickforce Studio, www.slickforce.com)

Thanks to dog wranglers: **Claire Doré** and **Jorgi Martin** and to **Mimi Green** dog collars.

Award-Winning Books & DVDs!

STEP-BY-STEP ACTIVITIES TO ENGAGE, CHALLENGE, AND BOND WITH YOUR DOG

Want more ways to have fun with your dog? Kyra Sundance's books and DVDs are beloved worldwide for their enthusiastic approach to dog training. Her straightforward step-by-step methods are accompanied by clear photos and video to make dog training a snap! Kyra's positive reinforcement methods instill a cooperative spirit in your dog and develop in them a love of learning.

Dog Training
Activity Kits

EVERYTHING INCLUDED

Each kit contains everything you need to be successful at teaching tricks to your dog. A step-by-step instruction booklet with clear photos makes training a snap! Open the box and you're ready to go!

DoMoreWithYourDog.com

DoMoreWithYourDog.com

ABOUT THE AUTHOR

KYRA SUNDANCE is a world-renowned dog trainer, lecturer, and internationally best-selling author. With over a million copies in print, Kyra's award-winning books, kits, and DVDs have inspired dog owners worldwide to develop fun and rewarding relationships with their dogs.

Honed through decades of professional experience, Kyra's easy-to-follow, step-by-step training methods are the most effective and humane way to train. Her positive methods foster confident, happy dogs who are motivated to do the right thing rather than fearful of making a mistake.

As professional performers, Kyra and her Weimaraners starred in shows for the king of Morocco, Disney's Hollywood stage shows, circuses, NBA halftime shows, on *The Tonight Show, Ellen, Animal Planet,* in movies, and in their own television series. Kyra is a professional set trainer for movie dogs and is nationally ranked in competitive dog sports. She presents workshops around the world on dog tricks and canine conditioning, where her enthusiasm inspires audiences to develop fun and rewarding relationships with their own dogs

Kyra is CEO of the Do More With Your Dog! trick dog titling organization, the National Trick Dog championships, and chair of the Trick Dog Expo.

An avid runner, Kyra competes in 35-mile (56 km) mountain ultramarathons and enjoys hanging out with her dogs and her rockstar husband, Randy, on their ranch in California's Mojave Desert.

Kyra

Can almost do a back handspring by herself if someone is spotting her.

kimba

Likes to take her Penguin Snuggy on hikes, to the mailbox, and on car rides.

Jadie

Has a hundred toys ... but probably still needs a few more.

DoMoreWithYourDog.com